RTI AND BEHAVIOR:

A Guide to
Integrating Behavioral
and
Academic Supports

Jeffrey Sprague
Clayton R. Cook
Diana Browning Wright
Carol Sadler

300280

LRP Publications
Horsham, Pennsylvania 19044

This publication was designed to provide accurate and authoritative information in regard to the subject matter covered. It is published with the understanding that neither the author nor the publisher is engaged in rendering legal, accounting, or other professional service. If legal advice or other expert assistance is required, the service of a competent professional should be sought.

Library of Congress Cataloging-in-Publication Data

RTI and behavior : a guide to integrating behavioral and academic supports / by Jeffrey Sprague . . . [et al.]
    p. cm.
   ISBN 1-57834-102-7
  1. Problem children--Education--United States. 2. Behavioral disorders in children--United States. 3. Learning disabled children--Education--United States. I. Sprague, Jeffrey R. (Jeffrey Richard), 1956-

  LC4802.R85   2008
  371.93--dc22

                        2008020780

About the Authors

JEFFREY SPRAGUE, Ph.D., is a professor of special education and director of the University of Oregon Institute on Violence and Destructive Behavior. He directs federal, state, and local research and demonstration projects related to positive behavior supports, response to intervention, youth violence prevention, alternative education, juvenile delinquency prevention, and school safety. His research activities encompass applied behavior analysis, positive behavior supports, functional behavioral assessment, school safety, youth violence prevention, and juvenile delinquency prevention. Dr. Sprague is a contributor to the federal government's *Early Warning, Timely Response* and the "President's Annual Report on School Safety," 1998 through 2000. He is author of the book, *CPTED for Schools: Crime Prevention Through Environmental Design* (National Clearinghouse for Educational Facilities, n.d.), written for school administrators. Dr. Sprague also is co-author of numerous articles and books, including a book he wrote with Hill Walker, *Safe and Healthy Schools: Practical Prevention Strategies* (Guilford Publications, 2005), and *Building Positive Behavior Support in Schools* (Sopris West, 2004), a book he authored with Annemieke Golly. He directs an R01 research grant from the National Institute on Drug Abuse to conduct the first evaluation of the effects of Positive Behavior Supports in middle schools. The study will assess the differential impact of intervention fidelity on antisocial behavior and substance use, and test a model of the influence of middle school discipline practices on the development of adolescent problems.

CLAYTON R. COOK, Ph.D., is an assistant professor of school psychology at Louisiana State University. He completed his doctoral training at the University of California, Riverside and internship at Boys Town in the Behavioral Pediatrics and Family Services Outpatient Clinic. He has extensive experience consulting with school staff to design and implement response to intervention models for academics and behavior. He has published several articles and delivered numerous presentations at national conferences on educational programming for students with emotional and behavioral problems. Dr. Cook's current research efforts are in the area of using RTI principles as a way of organizing and delivering services in restrictive settings to students with the most intense emotional and behavioral disorders.

DIANA BROWNING WRIGHT, M.S., L.E.P., is an educational and behavioral consultant who has been active in the field of general and special education, and psychology for 38 years. She is founder and director of the California Department of Education's Positive Environments, Network of Trainers (PENT, *www.pent.ca.gov*), and the Arizona Department of Education's Arizona High Achievement Academy (AHAA). She also is director of the Arizona Statewide Principals Institutes. A former teacher and school psychologist, Ms. Wright directs schools, districts, and regional and state improvement projects in educational reform related to academic achievement for diverse learners in elementary and secondary schools. She also consults with schools and school agencies on legally sound threat assessment procedures for general and special education students, response to aggressive and severe behavior, inclusive education, developmental assessment for intellectual disabilities, effective restrictive placements for E/BD students, functional behavior analysis and RTI for behavior. She is co-author of many research publications and manuals, including "Positive Interventions for Serious Behavior Problems," California's manual on functional assessment, the research-based *Behavior Support Plan Quality Evaluation Guide*, and *Behavior Support Plan Desk Reference*. In addition to consulting with educational agencies, she is an education consultant for LRP Publications and program advisor for LRP's National Institute on Legal Issues of Educating Individuals with Disabilities, where she annually presents on topics of national concern for special educators. Research endeavors and publications can be viewed at: *www.pent.ca.gov* and at *www.dianabrowningwright.com*.

iii

CAROL SADLER, Ph.D., is a school psychologist and retired school district administrator who currently works as a private consultant and trainer. During the last 15 years, she led and implemented a nationally recognized districtwide implementation of positive behavior support (PBS), which was enhanced in 2001 by a model demonstration grant she obtained from the U.S. Department of Education's Office of Special Education Programs for Effective Behavior and Instructional Support (EBIS). EBIS demonstrated how districts could implement a combined model of positive behavior support, school-wide reading, and use of student response to intervention for improving student outcomes across both general and special education. Through the efforts of Dr. Sadler and her colleagues, the district's EBIS model continues to have a positive influence on the work of schools, districts, and states throughout the country. Dr. Sadler has published several articles on leadership, implementation, and sustainability of the PBS and EBIS models, regularly assists schools and districts to implement these model practices, and is a frequent presenter at state and national conferences.

Table of Contents

Introduction

Despite facing dwindling resources and increasing legal challenges, educators are being held increasingly accountable for their efforts to ensure the academic, social and emotional well-being of their students. Moreover, legislation over the past few years has called for the use of proactive strategies to identify and serve students with academic and behavior problems. This changing accountability has been met by some resistance as schools continue to operate with outdated models of service delivery. Most schools, unfortunately, have not developed the systems capacity to meet these mandates. There is hope, however, in the procedures that constitute Response to Intervention (RTI). RTI provides a straightforward model of service delivery that includes procedures that allow educators to appropriately comply with legal mandates and at the same time ensure the academic, social and emotional well-being of their students.

RTI for behavior has emerged as a new way to think about early intervention assistance and disability identification for students with behavior problems who are at risk for developing emotional and behavioral disorders. RTI is the practice of matching high-quality, evidence-based interventions to student need, frequently monitoring student progress to make changes in intervention or goals, and applying student response data to make important educational decisions. The primary assumption under an RTI model is that different students will require instruction or behavioral supports of varying levels of intensity in order to experience success within school.

In its simplest expression, RTI involves documenting a change in behavior as a result of intervention. For example, the learner, while being provided with a particular level of instruction and support in an academic area, is periodically assessed and receives continued instruction and support that is adapted or intensified, depending on the assessment results. Similarly, a student who displays challenging behaviors is also repeatedly assessed, and, based on the results, the school staff uses scientifically validated practices to support the student in reducing those challenging behaviors and improving attitudes toward engagement in academic and social life. Once a student demonstrates an inadequate response to a series of intensifying interventions, the student can and should be given more intensive academic and/or behavioral support. This may include determining special education eligibility and related services, among other options (Gresham, 2004).

The RTI logic assumes that the severity of a student's difficulties can be evaluated by the degree to which he or she demonstrates an adequate or inadequate change in academic or behavioral performance as a function of being provided a scientifically based intervention (Gresham, 2002). Under such an approach, decisions regarding the intensity of an intervention necessary to meet a student's needs are based on how the student has responded to prior intervention attempts that have been implemented with integrity (consistently and as intended). Thus, student response is used as a basis to select, modify, intensify or lessen intervention strategies.

What This Book Provides

This book is designed to provide school administrators with the knowledge and skills needed to effectively implement an RTI approach for behavior. In so doing, this book addresses many of the practical questions related to the design and implementation of an RTI approach for behavior. We start by examining the origins and advantages of an RTI approach for behavior by discussing the limitations and problems of traditional models of assessment and service delivery, and scientific evidence supporting the use of RTI procedures for behavior. We then answer specific questions about implementing key components of an RTI model for behavior, including universal screening assessments, matching evidence-based and high-quality supports for students in each tier, continuous progress monitoring, data-based decision-making, and evaluation for special education services. The book includes a chapter describing a "real world" application of this approach in Oregon.

We end the book by addressing questions concerning the application of RTI procedures for behavior for students who already have an IEP, and offer a description of the legal and policy context for RTI and behavior support. We have provided numerous assessment tools and reproducible materials to assist in the direct implementation and training of RTI in your schools.

Chapter One

RTI for Behavior and Academic Supports: Building District- and School-level Capacity

After reading this chapter, you will be able to:

➢ give a rationale for integrating behavioral and academic support systems in schools;

➢ define RTI for behavioral support;

➢ describe six major components needed to install an effective and efficient multi-tiered behavioral support system at the district and school level; and

➢ provide strategies for ensuring adoption, implementation and maintenance of behavioral RTI systems.

Behavior Supports or Academics?

Many educators remark that intense federal and state requirements for demonstrating gains in academic achievement make it difficult to find time to focus on problem behaviors. Yet many students who misbehave also present serious learning challenges (Walker, Stieber, Ramsey, & O'Neill, 1993). In a misplaced attempt to be "fair" to typical students who are trying to learn, educators may be inclined to "punish" or exclude children who are acting out (Skiba, 2002).

Research strongly suggests that if schools raise their level of achievement, behavior decreases; and, if schools work to decrease behavior problems, academics improve (Hawkins, Catalano, Kosterman, Abbott, & Hill, 1999). So why not do both? Especially when we know that punishing the at-risk student populations and using "discipline" to systematically exclude them from schooling does not work. Schools that use office referrals, out-of-school suspension, and expulsion — without a comprehensive system that teaches positive and expected behaviors and rewards the same — are shown to actually have higher rates of problem behavior and academic failure (Mayer, Butterworth, Nafpaktitis, & Suzer-Azaroff, 1983). Specifically, chronic suspension and expulsion have detrimental effects on teacher-student relations, as well as on student morale; these kinds of responses leave the student with reduced motivation to maintain self-control in school, do not teach alternative ways to behave, and have been shown in the research to have limited effect on long-term behavioral adjustment. In fact, a history of chronic referrals, suspensions, and expulsions from school is a known risk factor for academic failure, dropout, and delinquency. There must be a better way.

Powerful longitudinal research shows that being engaged in schooling, bonding with teachers and other students, and experiencing academic success all serve as protective factors for students against a number of destructive outcomes, including school failure, delinquent acts, school dropout, and alcohol, tobacco and other drug use, to name a few (Gottfredson et al., 2000). Preventing such outcomes can begin with implementation of a multi-tiered model of positive behavior supports. When adopted and implemented, such supports serve the dual purpose of promoting protective factors for the majority of students and reclaiming others.

The Need for Integrated Behavioral and Academic Support Systems

More and more children and youth are bringing well-developed patterns of behavioral and academic adjustment problems to school. At-risk students often come to school with emotional and behavioral difficulties that interfere with their attempts to focus and learn (Reid, Patterson, & Snyder, 2002). Others may have interpersonal issues with other students or educators that make concentrating on learning difficult. Bullying, mean-spirited teasing, sexual harassment, and victimization are relatively common-place occurrences on school campuses, and these behaviors clearly compete with our schools' mission of closing the achievement gap!

Evidence-based best practice for supporting these students begins with identifying problems early, whether the problems are academic, emotional, behavioral, or interpersonal. After identification, interventions become essential to addressing the problem directly and thus reducing obstacles to successful school adjustment. If appropriate educational and behavioral supports were more widely provided, the long-term benefits would greatly exceed the costs (Alternbaugh, Engel, & Martin, 1995).

Basing Interventions on the Intensity of the Problem

The U.S. Public Health Service has developed a classification system of approaches to preventing problem behavior. This system has coordinated and integrated a range of interventions to address the needs of the three student types that are present in different proportions in every school: primary, secondary, and tertiary (Sprague & Walker, 2005). Primary prevention refers to the use of approaches that prevent problems from emerging; secondary prevention addresses the problems that already exist, but that are not yet of a chronic nature or severe magnitude; and tertiary prevention uses the most powerful intervention approaches available to address the problems of severely at-risk students. Hill Walker and his colleagues at the University of Oregon (Walker et al., 1996) outlined an integrated prevention model for schools that is based upon this classification system and addresses the problem of school-based emotional and behavior problems.

Universal interventions, applied at the primary prevention level to *all* students in the same manner and degree, are used to keep problems from emerging. Some good examples of such interventions include (a) developing a schoolwide discipline plan; (b) teaching conflict resolution and violence prevention skills to everyone; (c) establishing high and consistent academic expectations for all students; and (d) using the most effective, research-based methods for teaching beginning reading in the primary grades and supporting all students' reading performance throughout their school careers.

Individualized interventions, applied to one student at a time or to small groups of at-risk individuals (e.g., alternative classrooms or "schools within schools") are used to achieve secondary and tertiary prevention goals. Chronically at-risk students "select" themselves out by not responding well to primary prevention and need more intensive intervention services and supports if they are going to be able to change their problem behavior and achieve success within and beyond school. Often these interventions are made out to be too labor-intensive, complex, intrusive, and costly. In fact, many of the intensive, evidence-based interventions require low amounts of time from staff, cost little to no money to implement (e.g., self-monitoring, behavioral contracting, systematic school-home note system, check in/check out, and so forth), and they are necessary for delivering effective behavior supports.

As students move from primary prevention to secondary to tertiary supports, the intensity of assessment for intervention planning purposes increases. By the time the student has reached the level of tertiary prevention, a functional behavioral assessment process (FBA) is a necessary step to identify the conditions (e.g., antecedents and consequences) that sustain and motivate the problem behavior, and school personnel use that information to develop and implement individualized behavior support plans (O'Neill et al., 1997). A comprehensive assessment of family, school, and individual risk (e.g., family stressors, academic failure) and protective factors (e.g., gets along well with peers, controls impulses) also is invaluable in guiding the delivery of a broader system of interventions (Walker & McConnell, 1995).

This integrated model provides an ideal means for schools to develop, implement, and monitor a comprehensive management system that addresses the needs of all students in the school. In addition, the model has the potential to positively impact the operations, administration, and overall climate of the school. By emphasizing the use of universal interventions, this system makes the most efficient use of school resources and provides a supportive context for the application of necessary secondary and tertiary interventions for the more challenging students. Finally, it provides a built-in screening and assessment process; that is, by carefully monitoring students' responses to the primary interventions, it becomes possible to detect those who are at greater risk and in need of more intensive services, increasing the match between student need and intensity of support (Sprague, Sugai, & Walker, 1998). *This is known as Response to Intervention or RTI.*

What Is RTI?

In its simplest expression, RTI involves documenting a change in behavior or learning as a result of intervention (Gresham, 2004). For example, the learner, while being provided with a particular level of instruction and support in an academic area, is periodically assessed and receives continued evidence-based instruction and support that is adapted, intensified or withdrawn, depending on the assessment results. Similarly, a student who displays challenging behavior also is assessed, and, based on the results, receives evidence-based supports to reduce challenging behaviors and improve attitudes toward academic and social life.

The RTI approach to behavior support uses the identical three-tiered logic that has been adopted for literacy, and this ultimately simplifies the work of schools in both realms — academic and behavioral. If students are having a problem with learning, they are, more likely than not (and sooner or later), going to present problems in behavior, and vice versa. So the effort to screen and support early on both fronts becomes mutually serving for students, families, and educators. The mirrored three-tiered structures allow schools to continually monitor individual progress for behavioral and academic supports in an integrated and efficient fashion. It is close to self-defeating not to make a serious commitment to both. Clearly, integrating the approaches — from assessment to intervention to progress monitoring — makes the most sense. Figure 1, next page, (adapted from the National Center on Positive Behavior Interventions and Supports, *www.pbis.org*) illustrates the relationship between behavior and academics in the three-tiered approach.

Figure 1

Three-tiered Model of Behavioral and Academic Support Systems

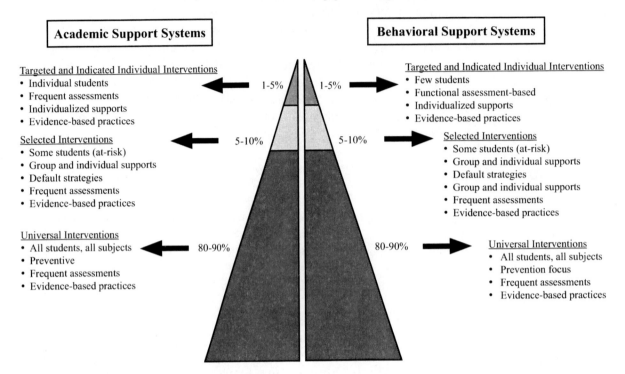

| Academic Support Systems | | Behavioral Support Systems |

Targeted and Indicated Individual Interventions
• Individual students
• Frequent assessments
• Individualized supports
• Evidence-based practices

1-5%   1-5%

Targeted and Indicated Individual Interventions
• Few students
• Functional assessment-based
• Individualized supports
• Evidence-based practices

Selected Interventions
• Some students (at-risk)
• Group and individual supports
• Default strategies
• Frequent assessments
• Evidence-based practices

5-10%   5-10%

Selected Interventions
• Some students (at-risk)
• Group and individual supports
• Default strategies
• Group and individual supports
• Frequent assessments
• Evidence-based practices

Universal Interventions
• All students, all subjects
• Preventive
• Frequent assessments
• Evidence-based practices

80-90%   80-90%

Universal Interventions
• All students, all subjects
• Prevention focus
• Frequent assessments
• Evidence-based practices

What Is RTI for Behavior?

RTI for behavior is the systematic process of providing a series of intensifying, evidence-based behavioral interventions and supports matched to student need. Student need is determined by inadequate response to an evidence-based, behavioral intervention implemented with fidelity (i.e., implemented as the program developers intended, right amount of lessons, etc.). RTI for behavior relies on the repeated collection of objective data (progress monitoring) to make decisions about whether the student is responding adequately or inadequately to the support(s) currently being provided.

The effectiveness of your RTI model for behavior support will depend on the quality of the interventions and supports that constitute the multiple tiers of support. Thankfully, many evidence-based interventions for behavior are available; they include methods based on applied behavior analysis (e.g., reinforcement), social learning (teaching expected behaviors through modeling and role playing), and cognitive behavioral methods to teach "thinking skills," such as problem-solving, impulse control, or anger management. The RTI focus on regular objective assessment helps us to decide whether to maintain, modify, intensify, or withdraw an intervention. Figure 2, next page, illustrates a sample "menu" of evidence-based interventions at each of the three-tiers. Each of the interventions listed in Figure 2 are shown to be effective in reducing problem behavior. You will be asked to build your own local RTI menu later in Chapter Three, and in Chapter Six we provide recommendations for selecting an appropriate mix of interventions based on legal and practical considerations.

Figure 2

Sample Intervention 'Menu' for Each Tier

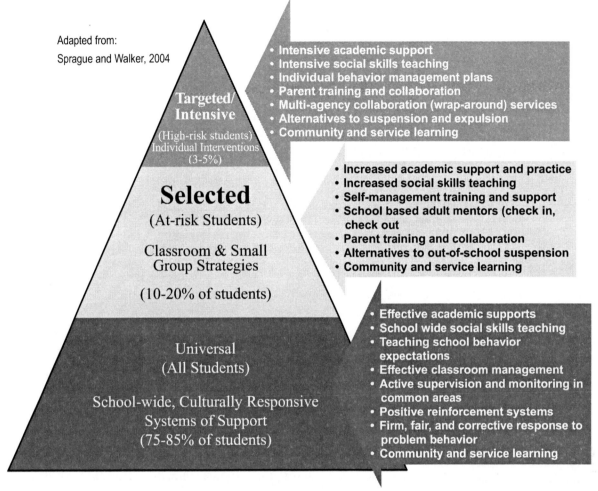

Adapted from:
Sprague and Walker, 2004

Targeted/Intensive
(High-risk students)
Individual Interventions
(3-5%)

- Intensive academic support
- Intensive social skills teaching
- Individual behavior management plans
- Parent training and collaboration
- Multi-agency collaboration (wrap-around) services
- Alternatives to suspension and expulsion
- Community and service learning

Selected
(At-risk Students)

Classroom & Small Group Strategies

(10-20% of students)

- Increased academic support and practice
- Increased social skills teaching
- Self-management training and support
- School based adult mentors (check in, check out
- Parent training and collaboration
- Alternatives to out-of-school suspension
- Community and service learning

Universal
(All Students)

School-wide, Culturally Responsive Systems of Support
(75-85% of students)

- Effective academic supports
- School wide social skills teaching
- Teaching school behavior expectations
- Effective classroom management
- Active supervision and monitoring in common areas
- Positive reinforcement systems
- Firm, fair, and corrective response to problem behavior
- Community and service learning

Frank Gresham published a seminal paper in the *Journal of School Psychology* outlining four major themes related to RTI and behavioral supports (Gresham, 2004). These themes provide the foundation concepts for this book and are described briefly below.

1. *Academic and behavioral interventions should be based on the intensity of the presenting problem.* The "three-tiered" approach to designing and selecting academic and behavioral supports involves providing supports at the universal level (all students), selected level (some students), and targeted/intensive level (a few students). At each subsequent tier, with fewer students and more intense problems, increasing levels of support are needed.

2. *RTI provides the basis for changing, modifying, or intensifying interventions.* Academic assessments are more commonly recognized and used in schools (e.g., reading fluency or comprehension, standardized test scores) to make data-based decisions regarding instruction. Similarly, systematically collected behavioral data (direct observations, office referral patterns, teacher ratings, points earned, etc.) provides a powerful basis for making decisions on behavior supports.

3. *Evidence-based practices are used in three ways:*

a. For selecting interventions;

b. For evaluating the effectiveness of an intervention; and,

c. For assessing the degree of fidelity with which it is applied (essentially, is it being used as it was designed to be used; is it being done right?).

This sets the stage for the necessary shift in schools from "paper implementation (e.g., revising policies, providing staff development)" to "process implementation (e.g., achieving effective and high-fidelity implementation of evidence-based supports that produce results)" involving high-quality supports and clear evidence that students are learning or their behavior is changing (Fixsen, Naoom, Blase, Friedman, & Wallace, 2005).

4. *Social validation is the final, critical component to implementing RTI and positive behavioral supports.* It requires that we ask every group of people affected by changes and improvements in systems and in student outcomes whether the approaches used, and the results, fit with their culture and values. It also requires, on the part of school staff, a consistent and sincere effort to keep students and families informed, involved, and invested in the outcomes relative to RTI practices.

Special Education Practices

Since the reauthorization of the Individuals with Disabilities Education Act in 2004, RTI has become a major stimulus for discussion and action. The language in IDEA focuses on RTI in relation to alternatives for identification and support of students with possible learning disabilities, and schools are increasingly adopting RTI logic to organize and deliver both academic and behavioral support for *all* students (Walker et al., 1996). This practice makes good sense. It certainly represents a more efficient use of resources. But there is another dimension that is perhaps even more important, one that stems from the common observation that many students struggle academically *and* exhibit problem behaviors. Simply, some students will misbehave because they "won't do it," and others will because they try and "cannot do it." But regardless of the emphasis, the fact remains that behavior and academic success are intimately connected and need to be intelligently addressed — together.

Why Is RTI Advocated as a Better Model?

Is RTI a better approach to address the social and behavioral needs of students than the traditional model of service delivery? Despite facing dwindling resources, educators are being held increasingly accountable for their efforts to ensure the academic, social, and emotional well-being of their students. Moreover, legislation over the past few years has called for the use of proactive strategies to identify and serve students with academic and behavior problems. This changing accountability has been met by some resistance as schools continue to operate with outdated models of service delivery. These schools have not developed the systems capacity to meet these mandates. There is hope, however, in the procedures that constitute RTI.

RTI provides a straightforward model of service delivery that includes procedures that allow schools to appropriately comply with legal mandates and at the same time ensure the academic, social, and emotional well-being of their students. An RTI model for behavior provides a fix for many of the problems inherent in the traditional model of service delivery. Perhaps the most significant limitation of the traditional model of service delivery is that it is reactive in addressing challenging behavior rather than proactive. This results in a "wait-to-fail" approach, whereby students (and their teachers) must struggle for a long period of time before they are assessed and provided assistance. This means that educators generally do not spring into action until the student's problems are pronounced and have been present for an extended period of time.

Under the traditional model, students are assumed to be performing well academically and behaviorally unless identified otherwise. The end result of this reactive approach is that many students fall through the cracks or develop deep-seated academic and behavioral problems that are resistant to remedial interventions and supports. Also, the traditional model of service delivery does not support the success of all students. It is exclusive in the sense that only those students who pass through the first gate — referral for problems — are even considered for psychological evaluation or extra behavior support. This is especially problematic in light of the research that indicates "teachers are imperfect tests" for identifying students for support (Gerber & Semmel, 1984; Gresham, MacMillan, & Bocian, 1997).

Research also suggests that schools vastly underserve the school-age population with emotional and behavioral problems (Walker, Nishioka, Zeller, Severson, & Feil, 2000). Specifically, more than 20 percent of the school-age population demonstrates deficits that would qualify them for a psychiatric diagnosis, but only 1 percent of the student population receives services under the category of emotional disturbance (ED) (Hoagwood, 1997). To make matters worse, for the 1 percent of students who eventually receive special education services under the Emotionally or Behaviorally Disturbed categories, services are often delayed until they reach middle or high school (Walker & Sylwester, 1991).

Adopting, Implementing and Maintaining RTI for Behavior: What Needs to Be in Place?

Schools that have high levels of collegiality, job control, and teacher participation in decision-making perform well in numerous respects. These conditions may lead to better adoption, implementation, and maintenance of RTI for behavior, provided the school embraces the goal of adopting RTI practices.

Bryk and Driscoll (1988) identified five features of the school "community" that appear to be associated with the general effectiveness of schools: (a) a system of shared values about the purpose of the school; (b) clear expectations for students and staff; (c) high expectations for student learning; (d) a common agenda of activities designed to foster meaningful social interactions among school members; and (e) social relations marked by caring. After controlling for a variety of differences in school characteristics, such as academic achievement and ethnic diversity, a composite "community index" was developed that included teacher satisfaction, staff morale, teacher and student absenteeism, student classroom disorder, student dropouts, and gain in academic achievement. Other studies also have shown greater gains in academic achievement in schools where faculty, students, and parents have participated in determining the goals and practices of the school. Such cooperative school environments are associated with higher levels of teachers' sense of efficacy and satisfaction as well.

Additionally, organizational effectiveness depends on (a) high-quality leadership and support provided by a principal or other administrator; (b) an internal "champion" for a program; (c) access to formal training and technical assistance; and (d) adequate financial resources for adoption, implementation, and maintenance of the program. Successful organization, implementation, and maintenance of prevention programs, in particular, have been shown to be related to principals' ability to (a) initiate and sustain innovation; (b) provide leadership in maintaining good relations with teachers, parents, school boards, site councils, and students (Gottfredson et al., 2000); and (c) provide support and encouragement to teachers delivering the program. Collectively, research studies support the importance of strong and consistent principal leadership as a critical component of getting an RTI model for behavior off the ground and sustaining it once it is up and running.

7

The availability of a strong program coordinator, or influential program champion, even without the support of a principal or agency director, also appears to be instrumental in determining whether an organization adopts, implements, and maintains an evidence-based prevention program. To increase the likelihood of success, there should be a program champion in every school where you are attempting to implement an RTI model for behavior.

Practices are more likely to be successfully implemented when teaching staff and administrators believe that the practices are effective, address a real problem, are worth the effort needed to implement, and will present no adverse side effects in the teaching environment. Mihalic and Irwin (Mihalic & Irwin, 2003) found that program features were the most important factors influencing the delivery and maintenance of eight different evidence-based programs; specifically, complex and/or poorly structured programs were subject to poor implementation practices.

Rogers' work on the diffusion of innovations (Rogers, 1995) suggests that the decision to adopt a program is influenced by program characteristics, such as the relative advantage of the proposed program to existing programs; its compatibility with existing values, previous experience, and current needs; the extent to which the program may be tested prior to adoption; and the extent to which the results of the program are publicly observable. Consistent with social marketing and DOI theory, information about the practice to be adopted must be persuasive and must link the advocated practices to valued outcomes that inform and motivate school staff (e.g., Rogers, 1995; Wallack, 1990).

RTI for behavior can move us closer to a vision of effective support for all students by helping us implement six essential concepts. These include (1) universal screening for behavioral adjustment, (2) continuous progress monitoring, (3) monitoring of intervention fidelity or quality, (4) data-based decision-making, (5) selecting evidence-based practices, and (6) providing multiple tiers of support. Each is defined below for the purposes of this chapter, the remainder of which will illustrate how each plays out in an RTI model for behavior.

> **Universal screening** — The systematic process of detecting a subset of students from the entire student population who are struggling academically and/or behaviorally, and at risk for experiencing a range of negative short- and long-term outcomes.

> **Progress monitoring** — The practice that is used to assess students' academic or behavioral performance and evaluate the effectiveness of instruction.

> **Intervention fidelity** — The notion that interventions or supports being implemented in an RTI model for behavior should be implemented as intended to enable appropriate and legally defensible decision-making.

> **Data-based decision-making** — A critical element of the problem-solving process that entails reviewing student response and intervention fidelity data in order to make decisions whether to maintain, modify, lessen, or intensify supports.

> **Evidence-based or scientifically validated interventions** — The idea that the interventions or supports implemented under an RTI model of behavior are supported by scientific research to improve student social and behavior functioning. Interventions or supports lacking scientific validation should not be considered for use.

> **Multiple tiers of behavior support** — The service delivery logic of providing a continuum of behavioral supports. This graduated sequence of intensifying interventions is used to match services and supports to student need.

Assessing District and School Capacity to Implement RTI for Behavior

An increasing number of systems' readiness checklists are becoming available as states, districts and schools prepare to implement RTI practices for general and special education decision-making in the area of academics (see Oregon Department of Education, 2005 for a good example). The Oregon document is modeled on the district example of Effective Behavior and Instructional Support featured in Chapter 6 of this guide (also see Sadler & Sugai, in press).

While the various RTI readiness checklists vary by degree, most identify essential systems' support features as including: (a) district leadership and commitment; (b) school leadership and collaborative, problem-solving teamwork; (c) universal screening and progress monitoring; (d) research-based and standards-driven curriculum, instruction and interventions; (e) coordination and coaching support; (f) professional development and capacity-building; (g) policies and procedures; and (h) visibility and political support.

Whether you are planning to focus your district's efforts on implementing RTI practices for academics, behavior, or a combination of both, you will find that the systems' support requirements are quite comparable. They will require your attention and will provide a framework for working with your fellow educators to create a common vision and action plan for your district. Figure 3 provides a comprehensive list of readiness items for you to use while assessing your capacity to adopt, implement and maintain integrated RTI systems for behavior support. We recognize that each school district and community will have different needs and resources, and that planning and implementation strategies will need to be tailored to those needs. You are encouraged to use this item list to create a checklist using a scale, such as "in place, in progress, or not started," and you also may choose to use the items to create a narrative list of goals and objectives related to each item or set of items.

* * * * * * * * * *

Figure 3

Response to Intervention Capacity Assessment Questions .

District-level leadership and commitment

- There is district-level support at the school board, superintendent, and administrative levels that includes an agreement to adopt, implement, and maintain an RTI approach.

- A district-level team is established with individuals who have expertise in developing, implementing, and sustaining a full range of behavior as well as academic interventions and supports.

- The team has a clear vision of how RTI, PBS and related practices fit within the larger context of their school improvement efforts.

- The district leadership team has defined a regular meeting schedule and meeting process (agenda, minutes, etc.).

- Capacity-building is facilitated through a rich variety of learning opportunities within and across schools (e.g., focused institutes, team meetings, study groups, site visits, etc.).

- The district and schools have defined policies, strategies, structures, roles and responsibilities in relation to RTI. They have a structure for monitoring fidelity of model implementation.

- There are individuals in the district and on the leadership team who are knowledgeable about effective professional development, systems' level planning, research-based curriculum and instructional practices, progress monitoring and data-based decision-making.

- A district-level coordinator(s) is identified who has adequate FTE to manage day-to-day operations.

- There is commitment to a long-term change process (3-5 years) evidenced by a multi-year prevention-focused action plan with goals, objectives, and action steps.

- The district is committed to providing adequate funding for curriculum and instruction, collaborative teamwork, professional development, technical assistance, and supplemental, instructional support.

- Resources are allocated for screening, progress monitoring, and interventions (personnel, time and materials).

- Social marketing and communication strategies have been identified and implemented to ensure that stakeholders are kept aware of activities and accomplishments (e.g., Web site, newsletter, conferences, TV).

- Trainers have been identified to build and sustain schoolwide RTI practices.

- District leadership has developed an evaluation process for assessing (a) extent to which teams are using schoolwide RTI, (b) impact of schoolwide RTI on student outcomes, and (c) extent to which the leadership team's action plan is implemented.

School leadership and collaborative, problem-solving teamwork

- Administrators and staff (general and special education) are willing to adopt RTI practices.

- An administrative leader (principal or associate principal) is an active member of the behavior support teams required for implementation at all tiers.

- Resources are committed at the school level to supporting collaborative, teacher collaboration for implementation of behavior supports.

- Evidence-based behavioral interventions at the primary, secondary, and tertiary levels have been identified and are in use.

- A coach is available to meet at least monthly with each emerging school team (emerging teams are teams that have not met the implementation criteria), and to meet at least quarterly with established teams.

- General education, special education, and compensatory education programs collaborate to support students and teachers.

- School-based information systems (e.g., data collection tools and evaluation processes) are in place.

Evidence-based core programs and integrated data systems

- With leadership and support from the district, the schools have adopted an integrated data system for universal screening and progress monitoring.

- Schools analyze and report data to regularly assess the effectiveness of core literacy, numeracy, and behavior support programs, and to select students for additional, supplemental instruction or intervention.

- Data-gathering and -use is geared to all students, including those with English as a second language.

- The district/schools have adopted evidence-based core programs for:

  ☐ ___Reading

  ☐ ___Writing

  ☐ ___Math

  ☐ ___Behavior Support

- The district/schools have developed systems and procedures for monitoring the fidelity of core and supplemental academic and behavioral interventions.

- The district and schools have developed systems for collecting and managing universal screening and progress monitoring data. The district provides ongoing training and coaching to ensure accuracy, reliability, and validity of data.

Universal screening and progress monitoring

- The schools have a student-level data collection and management system that is tied to behavioral interventions (e.g., *www.swis.org* or other system to track office discipline referrals).*

- The schools have defined systems for progress monitoring.

- Proactive, universal screening for externalizing and internalizing behavioral adjustment problems is conducted 2-3 times per year.

- Universal screening-data are shared from "sending" to "receiving" schools when students move from elementary to middle, and middle to high school.

Collaborative planning for supplemental interventions

- The schools have a team in place (e.g., Data Team, Behavior and Instructional Support Team) that includes representatives from all special and general education programs. This team leads the RTI implementation process.

- The schools have established procedures and provided necessary resources for grade-level teachers to meet regularly with the school leadership (aka Behavior and Instructional Support Team or data) team to plan, implement, and monitor students in supplemental intervention groups.

- The schools have access to a variety of evidence-based interventions and ongoing training to implement them. There are individuals who have expertise in action-research-design and effective use and progress monitoring of evidence-based and promising practices.

- The district and schools have developed standard protocols for reading and behavior, in particular, in order to improve effectiveness and efficiency of professional development.

- The schools are provided with additional training and support in teamwork techniques specific to efficient implementation of PBS and RTI, including effective collaboration, brainstorming, data-based decision-making and problem-solving.

- The schools are provided with personnel to assist in the ongoing management and implementation of instruction support (e.g., literacy specialists, counselors, learning specialists, ELL specialists, and educational/instructional assistants).

- School teams have developed and use generic (e.g., 80%/20% rule) and specific "Decision Rules" to guide changes in (intensify) instruction/ interventions.

- Teams have individuals who are knowledgeable about progress monitoring, including trend analysis, and instructional change techniques.

Individualizing and intensifying interventions

- The district and schools have developed procedures for individualizing, intensifying interventions for students who have not responded to supplemental group intervention.

- Individualizing and intensifying procedures include the following components:

  ☐ Procedures for gathering historical information (file reviews, developmental history),

  ☐ Procedures for examining LD "exclusionary" criteria,

  ☐ Forms for tracking student progress, especially those resulting in a referral for special education (as in 4B).

- The "Standard Protocol," especially for reading, includes clear guidelines for interventions at the "intensive" level, schedules for progress monitoring, and specific decision rules for determining whether or not to refer a student for special education evaluation, e.g., "dual discrepancy."

- School teams have access to, and ongoing training for implementing, a range of interventions for ruling in/out alternative explanations for a student's lack of progress; including interventions for LD, problems with attendance, cognitive ability, attention-control/health, sensory skills, language-related, and/or instruction-related causes.

- The district and schools have developed a standard protocol for functional behavioral assessment and linked behavior instruction plans.

- Teachers and team members receive regular training and support for implementation.

- The district has formalized points for parent involvement and consent within their RTI procedural guidelines.

Referral and evaluation for special education

- The district's special education manual includes specific guidance (Decision Rules) for evaluating a student's Response to Intervention (e.g., dual discrepancy and/or percentile cut-points).

- The district's special education manual includes all procedures, guidelines, and forms used in the RTI/evaluation process, including eligibility reporting formats.

- The district's special education manual provides guidance to school teams for evaluations under other special circumstances, such as dealing with private schools and other outside referrals, and reevaluations.

- The district's policies and procedures for special education evaluation and identification specify use of intensifying interventions and use of student response as a component of evaluation and identification of students with ED/EBD.

- The district's model for LD and ED/EBD evaluations is flexible to meet the needs of teams and students working at different grade levels. For example, at middle and high school a problem-solving team approach that starts by reviewing existing data and analyses of "strengths and weaknesses" may be appropriate.

References

Altenbaugh, R. J., Engel, D. E., & Martin, D. T. (1995). *Caring for kids: A critical study of urban school leavers*. Washington, D.C.: The Falmer Press.

Bryk, A. S., & Driscoll, M. E. (1988). The high school as community: Contextual influences and consequences for students and teachers.

Fixsen, G., Naoom, S. F., Blase, K. A., Friedman, R. M., & Wallace, F. (2005). *Implementation Research: A Synthesis of the Literature*. Tampa, FL: University of South Florida, Louis de la Parte Florida Mental Health Institute, The National Implementation Research Network (FMHI Publication #231).

Gerber, R., & Semmel, M. (1984). Teachers as imperfect tests: Reconceptualizing the referral process. *Educational Psychologist, 14*, 137-146.

Gottfredson, G. D., Gottfredson, D. C., Czeh, E. R., Cantor, D., Crosse, S. B., & Hantman, I. (2000). *National study of delinquency prevention in schools*. Ellicott City, MD: Gottfredson Associates.

Gresham, F. M. (2004). Current status and future directions of school-based behavioral interventions. *School Psychology Review, 33*(3), 326-343.

Gresham, F. M., MacMillan, D. L., & Bocian, K. (1997). Teachers as "tests": Differential validity of teacher judgments in identifying students at-risk for learning difficulties. *School Psychology Review, 26*, 47-60.

Hawkins, J. D., Catalano, R. F., Kosterman, R., Abbott, R., & Hill, K. G. (1999). Preventing adolescent health-risk behaviors by strengthening protection during childhood. *Archives of Pediatrics & Adolescent Medicine, 153*, 226-234.

Hoagwood, K. E. (1997). Effectiveness of school-based mental health services for children: A 10-year research review. *Journal of Child and Family Studies, 6*(4), 435-451.

Mayer, G. R., Butterworth, T., Nafpaktitis, M., & Suzer-Azaroff, B. (1983). Preventing school vandalism and improving discipline: A three year study. *Journal of Applied Behavior Analysis, 16*, 335-369.

Mihalic, S. F., & Irwin, K. (2003). *Blueprints for violence prevention: From research to real world settings — Factors influencing the successful replication of model programs: Youth Violence and Juvenile Justice*.

O'Neill, R. E., Horner, R. H., Albin, R. W., Sprague, J. R., Newton, S., & Storey, K. (1997). *Functional assessment and program development for problem behavior: A practical handbook*. (Second ed.). Pacific Grove, CA: Brookes/Cole Publishing.

Oregon Department of Education (2005). Response to intervention readiness checklist. Available at *http://www.ode.state.or.us/initiatives/idea/orrtitreadinesschecklist.doc*.

Reid, J., Patterson, G., & Snyder, J. (2002). *Antisocial behavior in children and adolescents: A developmental analysis and model for intervention*. Washington, DC: American Psychological Association.

Rogers, E. M. (1995). *Diffusion of innovations*. New York: The Free Press.

Skiba, R. J. (2002). Special education and school discipline: A precarious balance. *Behavior Disorders, 27*(81-97).

Sprague, J., Sugai, G., & Walker, H. M. (1998). Antisocial behavior in schools. In S. M. Watson & F. M. Gresham (Eds.), *The handbook of child behavior therapy*. New York: Plenum Press.

Sprague, J. R., & Walker, H. M. (2005). *Safe and healthy schools: Practical prevention strategies*. New York: Guilford Press.

Walker, H. M., Horner, R. H., Sugai, G., Bullis, M., Sprague, J. R., Bricker, D., et al. (1996). Integrated approaches to preventing patterns among school-age children and youth. *Journal of Emotional & Behavioral Disorders, 4*(4), 194-209.

Walker, H. M., Nishioka, V. M., Zeller, R., Severson, H. H., & Feil, E. G. (2000). Causal factors and potential solutions for the persistent under-identification of students having emotional or behavioral disorders in the context of schooling. *Assessment for Effective Intervention, 26*, 29-40.

Walker, H. M., & McConnell, S. R. (1995). *The Walker-McConnell scale of social competence and school-adjustment (SSCSA)*. San Diego, CA: Singular Publishing Group.

Walker, H. M., Sieber, S., Ramsey, E., & O'Neill, R. E. (1993). Fifth grade school adjustment and later arrest rates: A longitudinal study of middle school antisocial boys. *Journal of Child & Family Studies, 2*(4), 295-315.

Walker, H. M., & Sylwester, R. (1991). Where is school along the path to prison? *Educational Leadership, 49*(1), 14-16.

Chapter Two

Universal Screening: Finding the 'Right' Customers for Additional Supports

After reading this chapter, you will be able to:

➤ describe the importance of universal screening within an RTI model for behavior and how it aligns with federal legislation and best practice;

➤ discuss different universal screening methods that are available to identify students in need of additional positive behavior supports;

➤ describe how to implement a universal screening system in your schools; and

➤ illustrate a real-world application of universal screening for behavior problems.

Imagine for a just moment that you have a three-tier model of positive behavior supports up and running in your schools, and every student is being exposed to an array of universal (Tier 1) positive behavior supports. According to the research and our experience, you can expect somewhere between 10 percent to 20 percent of your students will continue to engage in challenging behaviors despite the implementation of universal, schoolwide supports. Will you withhold additional services for students who continue to exhibit challenging behaviors, despite your best efforts? Will you wait until their behaviors become so problematic that they create disorderly and unsafe learning environments, and staff can no longer tolerate them? The answer to this question seems obvious, since it is hard to envision anyone in education who would outwardly endorse such a reactive approach to addressing behavior problems. But the irony is that school personnel take this approach all too often. If you see the glaring problems in this approach and would rather act proactively to address students' behavior problems before they become entrenched and lead to long-term adjustment problems, then you need a method of identifying students struggling with behavioral issues early on and throughout the academic year to provide them with more intensive positive behavior supports. How, then, can you proactively identify these students to provide them with more intense services? The answer to this question is a universal screening system. Universal screening is the process of proactively finding the "right" students — those who need additional positive behavior supports.

Universal Screening: Purpose, Law and Best Practice

Many other fields have well-established universal screening practices to identify problems early on and provide effective treatment (supports) before the problems develop into more problematic conditions, diseases, or disorders. The field of medicine, for example, has several screening tests to detect cancer before it metastasizes. Specifically, there is the prostrate-specific antigen (PSA) test to screen for prostate cancer, the mammogram test to detect breast cancer, and the Papanicolaou (Pap) test to identify cervical cancer in its early stages (Walker, Ramsay, & Gresham, 2005). Despite knowing a great deal about the factors that predict whether a student is at risk for developing later emotional and behavioral disorders, the field of education has been very slow to adopt universal screening procedures. Indeed, a seminal article written by James Kauffman in 1999 stated that educators actually "prevent prevention" of emotional and behavioral disorders through well-intended efforts to guard students from the perceived

17

negative effects of labeling and stigmatization associated with screening and identification. The problem in this way of thinking is that if students with behavior problems do not receive intervention and supports, then there is good chance they will continue to display some degree of problem behavior throughout their lives (Bullis & Walker, 1994; Kazdin, 1987; Patterson, Reid, & Dishion, 1992).

The philosophy underlying universal screening represents a significant departure from the traditional approach to service delivery. The traditional approach to delivering services to students at risk for emotional and behavioral disorders consists of teacher referral, psychoeducational testing, and special education placement. This is commonly referred to as the refer-test-place model of service delivery, and it parallels practices for identifying students with learning disabilities. A teacher initiates the process by referring a student to the administration or school psychologist once the student's behaviors have exceeded his/her patience and tolerance level. Unfortunately, research indicates that teachers are "imperfect tests" when they are not given a systematic procedure to follow (Gerber & Semmel, 1984; Gresham, MacMillan, & Bocian, 1997). This leaves the referral process susceptible to negative influences, such as reputational bias; racial or other stereotypes; personality conflicts; or individual teacher tolerance levels and personal agendas. There is a solution to these problems — a systematic process for screening all students according to data-based criteria.

Education professionals have historically been reactive in the provision of early intervention and remediation supports. This is tantamount to a "wait-to-fail" approach, whereby students must struggle behaviorally for years before they are referred for extra supports and services. Indeed, national data on special education identification rates indicate that the majority of students with emotional and behavioral problems are identified as emotionally disturbed between 13 and 15 years old. Universal screening within an RTI model for behavior does away with the "wait-to-fail" phenomenon, because it is naturally a prevention-focused endeavor. That is, all the students are proactively screened at regularly scheduled time points throughout the year to identify a select group of students who demonstrate early behavioral warning signs that indicate risk for developing a bona fide emotional or behavioral disorder and portend negative life course outcomes. Thus, rather than wait years for a student to fail, RTI assumes that if students who are identified by the universal screening process continue to demonstrate an inadequate response to a sequence of intensified, evidenced-based behavior supports, then that student can and should be given more intensive intervention assistance including, but not limited to, special education and related services (Gresham, 2004).

The idea that students will outgrow their behavior problems is a myth, since the most potent predictor of later behavior problems is previous behavior problems (Lipsey & Derzon, 1998). Therefore, students who engage in behavior problems are likely to continue to engage in behavior problems in the absence of additional support. Taking this into mind, it is in the best interest of students and staff to engage in systematic screening efforts to identify those students who display emerging patterns of behavior problems to prevent subsequent behavior problems and the host of negative outcomes that may follow suit. Universal screening allows your staff to act in a proactive manner to address student behavior problems, rather than waiting to a point where students' behavior problems have become so entrenched that they will likely be non-responsive to the most well-thought out, well-implemented, and well-intended interventions (Kazdin, 1987).

Universal screening is supported by federal legislation governing educational practice. For example, the No Child Left Behind Act (2001) includes specific language endorsing universal screening to identify students at risk for school failure. Also, the Individuals with Disabilities Education Act (2004) delineates requirements for early child find and screening for disabilities. Moreover, the President's Commission on Excellence in Special Education has called for the early identification and intervention of students who are experiencing academic and behavioral problems. In addition to federal legislation, the National Association of School Psychologists, American Psychological Association, and the National Association of State Directors of Special Education, all well-respected organizations in the field, provide unambiguous endorsement for the use of universal screening procedures as part of the delivery of preventive and remedial services. Universal screening also is considered best practice among researchers in the early identification and prevention of emotional and behavioral disorders (Conroy, Hendrickson, & Hester, 2004; Smith & Fox, 2003; Walker, Ramsay, & Gresham, 2005).

Universal screening within an RTI approach to behavior helps fulfill "child find" obligations for determining who requires special education services. Students who exhibit problem behaviors need to be located and served in order to remove barriers to educational success. When a school and district systematically locate behavior problems in public and private schools, and then respond with interventions, a first step in child find has begun. Behavior problems left untreated can result in reduced academic success, as well as continue in severity until an emotional behavioral disorder is present. The IDEA "child find" provisions (20 USC 1412(a), 34 CFR 300.111) require every state to adopt policies and procedures so that all children with disabilities residing in the state (including children with disabilities who are homeless, wards of the state, or attending private schools) regardless of the severity of their disabilities, and who are in need of special education and related services, are "identified, located and evaluated." The state's child find process also must include children who are suspected of being a student with a disability and in need of special education, even though they are advancing from grade to grade. 34 CFR 300.111(c)(1). Through systematic universal screening to determine who needs additional services and supports, the IDEA mandate to find the children with disabilities is fulfilled. Those who do not respond may, in fact, have an, as of yet, undiscovered disability requiring further assessment. (For more on child find as it relates to RTI, see Chapter 1 of *What Do I Do When . . . The Answer Book on RTI*, LRP Publications Inc., 2007.)

In sum, schools have historically made it their primary mandate to ensure the academic success of all students. Whereas, schools continue to relegate the social, emotional, and behavioral welfare of students to a secondary mandate that often is ignored and goes unfulfilled. It is about time that educators recognize that academic and behavior adjustment are intimately intertwined. Recognition of this will help expand the mission of schools to include the social, emotional, and behavioral development of all students. By adopting universal screening procedures for behavior problems, you are taking a giant step toward integrating the social, emotional, and behavioral development of students as a critical component of the provision of educational services and care in your schools. Now that you are well aware of the importance of universal screening, you probably are eager to know what universal screening methods are available and how you use them to improve outcomes for students.

Multiple Gating

The first universal screening method you should consider using is multiple gating. Research has established multiple gating as a reliable and valid set of screening procedures for identifying students at risk for subsequent emotional and behavior disorders. Multiple gating refers to a process in which a series of progressively more costly, time-intensive and precise assessments (i.e., gates) are used to identify students who are in need of more intensive services and supports (Feil, Severson, & Walker, 2002; Loeber, Dishion, & Patterson, 1984; Walker & Severson, 1990). Multiple gating begins by considering the entire student body and finishes with a select group of students with behavior problems who have been unresponsive to universal supports and, therefore, are at increased risk for experiencing continued short- and long-term negative outcomes.

The feature that distinguishes multiple gating from other screening approaches is that it minimizes classification errors via a multi-informant, multi-method approach. Multiple gating, therefore, will help your staff members hold the number of false positives (students identified as positive for more intensive services but in reality do not need them) and false negatives (students identified as negative for more intensive supports but in reality do need them) to a minimum. Errors are a reality in any classification system. However, not all classification errors are created equal, since you would be better off saying a student needs more intensive supports only to find out that s/he does not (false positive), than failing to provide more intensive supports to a student who is in need of them (false negative).

A multiple-gating procedure fits seamlessly within a multi-tiered system of service delivery. It represents the bridge that students travel to get from Tier I to Tier II positive behavior supports. Said another way, multiple gating is the process by which students are identified as at risk for developing an emotional and behavioral disorder and, thus, placed within a tier of more intensive services. When multiple gating is performed correctly, 10 percent to 20 percent of the total student population will be identified as continuing to have behavior problems despite the implementation of Tier I positive behavior supports — i.e., inadequate response to intervention.

The most well-known and researched multiple-gating system is Walker and Severson's (1990) *Systematic Screening for Behavioral Disorders* (SSBD). The SSBD has been used and validated in numerous studies to screen elementary-age children for behavior problems. The SSBD takes students through three progressive and more precise assessment phases called gates: Gate 1: out of all students in a class, teacher nominates and rank-orders students along specified criteria; Gate 2: out of all the nominated students, teachers complete norm-referenced checklists to quantify behaviors and identify students who exceed normative cutoff points; and Gate 3: out of students who exceed normative cutoff, support staff (e.g., school psychologists or counselors) directly observe students in their natural environments. The SSBD uses traditional assessment tools (teacher nominations, Likert ratings, systematic direct observations) that are likely familiar to you and your staff and incorporates systematic data-based decision-making according to specific screening criteria and cutoff points. The cutoff points for Gates 2 and 3 are based on a large national standardization sample including nearly 6,000 students. Figure 1, next page, illustrates this process.

Figure 1

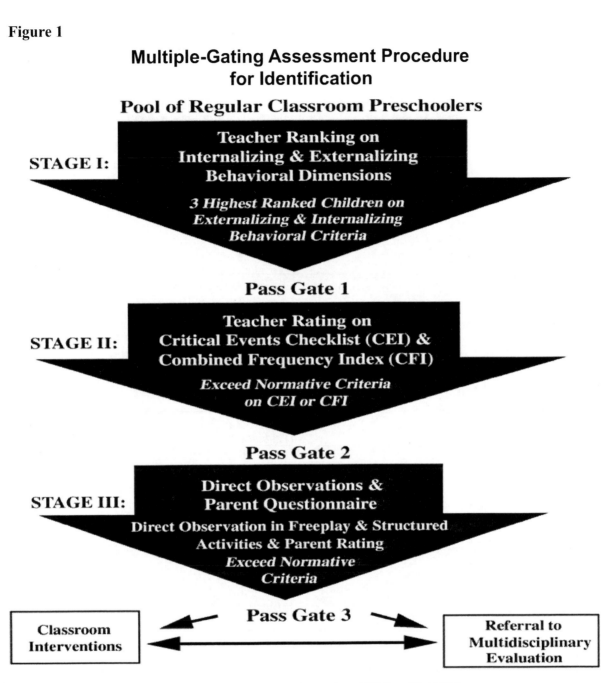

Multiple-Gating Assessment Procedure for Identification

Pool of Regular Classroom Preschoolers

STAGE I: Teacher Ranking on Internalizing & Externalizing Behavioral Dimensions

3 Highest Ranked Children on Externalizing & Internalizing Behavioral Criteria

Pass Gate 1

STAGE II: Teacher Rating on Critical Events Checklist (CEI) & Combined Frequency Index (CFI)

Exceed Normative Criteria on CEI or CFI

Pass Gate 2

STAGE III: Direct Observations & Parent Questionnaire

Direct Observation in Freeplay & Structured Activities & Parent Rating *Exceed Normative Criteria*

Pass Gate 3

Classroom Interventions

Referral to Multidisciplinary Evaluation

Adapted from: Feil, E., Severson, H. and Walker, H. (1994),
Early screening project: Identifying preschool children with adjustment problems.
The Oregon Conference Monograph, Vol. 6.

Gate 1

The first step in the SSBD multiple gating requires all general education teachers to systematically assess the behavioral features of all students in their classrooms and rank order them according to two distinct behavioral profiles: externalizing and internalizing behaviors. Externalizing behaviors are under-controlled behaviors that are directed outward to the social environment and disruptive in nature, including aggression, fidgeting, talking out loud, hyperactivity, and property damage. Internalizing behaviors, on the other hand, are over-controlled, covert behaviors that are directed inward from the social environment and difficult to detect, such as depression, social avoidance, anxiety, and phobias. The top three to five students in each class (6 to 10 total) exhibiting behaviors that are consistent with profiles of externalizing and internalizing patterns of behavior pass through Gate 1 and move on to the next assessment stage in the multiple-gating process. Figure 2 provides a sample teacher nominating form.

Figure 2

Teacher Nomination Sample

Examples of externalizing types of behavior	Examples of internalizing types of behavior
Displaying aggression toward objects or persons	Low or restricted activity levels
Arguing or defying the teacher	Avoidance of speaking with others
Forcing the submission of others	Shy, timid, and/or unassertive behaviors
Out-of-seat behavior	Avoidance or withdrawal from social situations
Noncompliance with teacher instructions or requests	A preference to play or spend time alone
Tantrums	Acting in a fearful manner
Hyperactive behavior	Avoiding participation in games and activities
Disturbing others	Unresponsive to social interactions by others
Stealing	Failure to stand up for oneself
Not following teacher or school rules	
Non-examples of externalizing types of behavior	**Non-examples of internalizing types of behavior**
Cooperating	Initiation of social interactions with peers
Sharing	Engagement in conversations with peers
Working on assigned tasks	Normal rates or level of social contact with peers
Asking for help	Displaying positive social behaviors toward others
Listening to teacher	Participating in games and activities
Interacting in appropriate manner with peers	Resolving peer conflicts in an appropriate manner
Following directions	Joining in with others
Attending to task demands	
Complying with teacher requests	
Student Nomination	
Externalizing Students	**Internalizing Students**
1	1
2	2
3	3
4	4
5	5

Gate 2

The second stage of assessment involves the use of brief, user-friendly teacher ratings of maladaptive and adaptive behaviors — the Combined Frequency Index and the Critical Events Index — to establish which students are exhibiting the most symptomatic behaviors of an underlying emotional and behavioral disorder. The Combined Frequency Index assesses how often the student engages in common adaptive and maladaptive behaviors, while the Critical Event Index includes 33 items that measure low-frequency, high-intensity behaviors that have been termed "behavioral earthquakes" given the serious implications they have for a child's future outcomes (e.g., fire setting, use of weapons, suicidal ideation, severe depression, self-abuse, and encopresis). Students who exceed normative criteria on these scales pass through Gate 2 and are involved in stage 3 of assessment in the SSBD multiple-gating process.

Gate 3

The purpose of the third stage of assessment is to provide direct assessments of student behavior in natural educational environments. The SSBD includes two direct observation coding protocols: The Peer Social Behavior Code (PSB), which is used to record playground behavior and the Academic Engaged Time Code (AET), which is used to record classroom behavior. Observations are conducted by support staff, such as a school psychologist, school counselor, special educator, behavior specialist or school social worker. For each setting, two 15-minute observations are conducted on different days to generate an estimate of the student's typical behavior on the playground and in the classroom. The SSBD training manual includes quizzes and a video to practice learning how to competently complete the observational system.

The purpose of the PSB Observation is to assess the students' social behavior during recess periods. Observers record behavior according to four behavioral categories: (1) *Social Engagement* (SE) — exchange of verbal or non-verbal social signals between two or more children; (2) *Participation* (P) — when child participating in game/activity with set rules, with one or more children; (3) *Alone* (A) — when child is not within five feet of another student and not socially engaged; and (4) *Parallel Play* (PLP) — when child is engaged in activity that falls within five feet of another student, but there is no interaction (verbally or non-verbally) with her/him. Scoring the PSB data requires dividing the total number of intervals that were observed during a session by the intervals recorded under different categories. These numbers are then multiplied by 100 to provide an estimate of the percent of time the student engaged in each behavior category.

The AET Observation Code measures a student's engagement in the academic setting. Academic engaged time has been found to be a strong predictor of academic success and a student's adjustment to the demands of academic settings (DiPerna, Volpe, & Elliott, 2002). AET refers to the amount of time a student spends engaged on academic tasks. The person observing the student uses a stopwatch to record the total amount of time a student maintains engagement in academic tasks. The observer simply starts the watch when the student is engaged in the academic task and stops it when the student disengages. AET is computed by dividing the time recorded on the stopwatch by the total amount of time of the observation and then multiplying it by 100. This will provide the percent of time during the observation period that the student was academically engaged. The students' data are then compared to normatively derived cutoff points (Walker & Severson, 1990). Students who exceed normative cutoff points are considered at risk for EBD and in need of additional positive behavior supports.

Early Screening Project

The notion of early identification and intervention of behavior problems in children between the ages of 3 to 5 is based on the assumption that early screening, prevention, and intervention can prevent later problems, such as academic failure, crime, mental health problems, unemployment and substance abuse. There is convincing research on the benefits of early intervention to improve the educational, social, and vocational outcomes of students (Zigler, Taussig, & Black, 1992).

With this in mind, Hill Walker, Herbert Severson, and Edward Feil developed The Early Screening Project (ESP). The ESP is a downward extension of the SSBD that enables school personnel to identify children between the ages of 3- to 5-years-old with budding patterns of behavior problems to provide them preventive supports and services. The ESP is in alignment with IDEA 2004 child find obligations. Like the SSBD, the ESP screens for and finds both acting-out/externalizing and withdrawn/internalizing behavior patterns. The ESP screening process consists of three increasingly refined stages of assessment, consisting of teacher nominations, teacher ratings, and direct observations of behavior.

Universal Screening Scales

Drummond (1994) developed a highly accurate, brief, free universal screener that relies on teachers' judgment of students' risk status for antisocial behavior. The Student Risk Screening Scale (SRSS) is a one-page instrument that lists all the students in the class in the first column and seven rating items across the top row: (1) stealing, (2) lying, cheating, sneaking, (3) behavior problems, (4) peer rejection, (5) low academic achievement, (6) negative attitude, and (7) aggressive behaviors. The teacher evaluates and assigns a frequency-based, 4-point Likert rating to each student in the class for each of the seven behavior rating items. Total scores on the SRSS can range from 0 to 21 with scores of 9–21 indicating high risk, 4–8 indicating moderate risk, and 0–3 defining low-risk status. The SRSS is an excellent tool to use in initial screening when you are seeking to proactively detect students with emerging externalizing or antisocial behavior patterns. The SRSS, however, was not developed to screen and identify students who are withdrawn, anxious, or depressed. Figure 3, next page, illustrates the Drummond universal screening form.

Figure 3

Student Risk Screening Scale (SRSS) (Drummond, 1994)

Directions: Please rate each student on each behavior using the following scale:
0=Never, 1=Rarely, 2=Occasionally, 3=Frequently

Student Name	Stealing	Lying, Cheating, Sneaking	Behavior Problems	Peer Rejection	Low Academic Achievement	Negative Attitude	Aggressive Behaviors

Given that a companion universal screener to the SRSS does not exist to identify students at risk for developing an internalizing behavior disorder, the authors developed the Student Internalizing Behavior Screening Scale (SIBSS). Consistent with the SRSS, seven items were drawn from the research base as risk factors for developing an internalizing behavior disorder. Teachers rate each student in the class on the following seven items: (1) nervous or fearful, (2) bullied by peers, (3) spends time alone, (4) low academic achievement, (5) withdrawn, (6) sad or unhappy, and (7) complains about being sick or hurt. Figure 4, next page, illustrates the SIBSS. Unlike the SRSS, the SIBSS has not yet been empirically evaluated as a reliable and valid universal screener. However, the second author is currently in the process of doing so. If you choose to use the SIBSS, you will want to compare the data with data derived from other established methods.

Figure 4

Student Internalizing Behavior Screening Scale (SIBSS)

Directions: Please rate each student on each behavior using the following scale:
0=Never, 1=Rarely, 2=Occasionally, 3=Frequently

Student Name	Nervous or fearful	Bullied by peers	Spends time alone	Low academic achievement	Withdrawn	Sad or unhappy	Complains about being sick or hurt

Office Discipline Referrals

Office discipline referrals (ODRs) serve as another potential source of data to use for universal screening purposes. An office discipline referral should be issued by school staff for serious behavioral violations, such as fighting, noncompliance, property damage, bullying, or harassment, not for minor behavior problems, such as off-task behavior, mild disruptive classroom behavior, mild negative social interactions. ODR data are collected and summed for each student throughout the academic year. Researchers have established cutoffs to determine responsiveness to schoolwide positive behavior supports. Students who receive 0 to 1 ODRs during the academic year are considered to be adequate responders to the schoolwide, universal positive behavior supports and, thus, not in need for more intensive supports at Tiers II and III. Whereas, students who receive two or more ODRs within the academic year are deemed to have problem behavior that is not fully responsive to the schoolwide supports. Therefore, these students are in need of more intensive supports beyond what is provided on a schoolwide basis. The primary limitations of ODR data are that it misses minor behavior violations and does not capture students with internalizing behavior problems.

Additional Universal Screening Considerations

Once you have carefully selected the universal screening method that best fits your schools' needs, the next step is to determine the number of times students will be screened each year. On the academic side of the equation, Curriculum-Based Measurement (CBM) has been used to conduct universal screening. Best practice is to administer CBM probes three times per academic year to identify those students who are performing below the 25th percentile on grade-level probes. The standard is to allow two to three months to elapse before performing the initial universal screening, and every two months thereafter (see Table 1 below for example timeline). This allows school staff sufficient time to get to know the students, and students the opportunity to demonstrate adequate or inadequate response to the Tier I supports. Screening on the behavior side can and should be integrated with academic screening. You can set aside time to conduct both academic and behavior screening at predetermined time points during the academic year. This way you can systematically identify those students in need of more intensive academic supports, positive behavior supports, or both.

Table 1

Example Universal Screening Timeline

Tasks	Dates	Universal Screening Steps
Universal Screening 1	Week of October 22 - 26	
Teacher nominations	October 22	All general education teachers rank order students
Administer Rating scales	October 23	School team gives rating scales to teachers to complete
Score rating scales	October 24	School team collects and scores rating scales
Conduct observations	October 24 & 25	School team members conduct observations
Selection of Tier II Students	October 26	School team members review data and select students
Universal Screening 2	Week of January 7 - 11	
Teacher nominations	January 7	All general education teachers rank order students
Administer Rating scales	January 8	School team gives rating scales to teachers to complete
Score rating scales	January 9	School team collects and scores rating scales
Conduct Observation	January 10	School team members conduct observations
Selection of Tier II Students	January 11	School team members review data and select students
Universal Screening 3	Week of March 17 - 21	
Teacher nominations	March 17	All general education teachers rank order students
Administer Rating scales	March 18	School team gives rating scales to teachers to complete
Score rating scales	March 19	School team collects and scores rating scales
Conduct Observation	March 20	School team members conduct observations
Selection of Tier II Students	March 21	School team members review data and select students

You also will want to consider how many students your schools are capable of effectively supporting in the higher tiers of positive behavior support. It may be the case, given limited staff and resources, that you can only accommodate 5 percent to 10 percent of the student population in Tiers II and III. This obviously will affect the decisions you make and students who are ultimately identified when conducting universal screening. All the screening procedures discussed above can be adjusted to fit your needs, as you will see in the discussion below on the real world application of universal screening. We recommend triaging students based on universal screening data. Thus, the students are ranked from most to least at risk, and depending on how many students can be served, the top 5 percent to 10 percent of students are considered for more intensive, positive behavior supports.

29

You also must be aware of the fact that classification errors are a reality of any screening system — you inevitably will be confronted with students who you missed or accidentally provided more intensive services even though they did not need them. The advantage of an RTI approach, however, is that it is flexible, allowing students to move throughout tiers based on their response to intervention. Therefore, if a student is not detected by the screening process but exhibits behaviors that necessitate more intensive supports, the school team has the option of collecting additional data on the student (e.g., records review, interview, observation, testing, and/or scales) to justify the need for more intensive services. In a similar way, if a student is identified by the screening system as an inadequate responder, but progress-monitoring data indicate no behavior problems from the outset of the supplemental behavior program, then the school team can make the data-based decision to lower the student back down to Tier I.

A critical feature of being an effective educator is "flexibility." *Merriam-Webster's Dictionary* defines flexibility as a "ready capability to adapt to new, different, or changing requirements." To be a flexible educator means that you must be able to adapt and address different circumstances that seemingly arise out of thin air. One circumstance that inevitably will occur that will require you to be flexible with your universal screening system is students who engage in significant problem behavior prior to one of the dates scheduled for universal screening. In this circumstance, you are confronted with the dilemma of waiting for the universal screening date to arrive to determine the student's need for more intense services or acting in a responsive manner to the presenting problem. In the spirit of flexibility, the school team should reserve the right to consider a student for additional positive behavior supports outside of the universal screening protocol. This decision, like all others under an RTI framework, is data-based, so you are confident that, indeed, more intensive services are warranted.

The school team has the responsibility to ensure that this option is not abused by teachers or other school staff. You can easily imagine the stress that certain students create for teachers. This stress sometimes has a way of motivating teachers to refer students to the school team for the sole purpose of getting them removed from their class. How do you make sure this option is not abused? The first step is to make sure the Tier I supports are being implemented accurately and consistently. In order to appropriately assess RTI, there has to be high-quality supports in place to which the student would either respond adequately or inadequately. Also, if multiple students in a particular class are engaging in problem behavior, then this is a good sign that what you have on your hands is a teacher problem, not a student problem. In this case, you will want to work with the teacher on implementing the universal behavior supports appropriately before you consider the students in this class for additional positive behavior supports. Second, a single episode of problem behavior — one bad day — should not warrant consideration for Tier II supports. Although the episode may have involved disrespectful and difficult to tolerate behavior, you want to be careful not to jump the gun. Be patient, because if the episode is a sign of what is to come, then the subsequent behaviors will provide the data needed to justify more intensive services.

Real-World Application of Universal Screening within an RTI Model for Behavior

The following is a discussion of a real-world application of universal screening within an RTI model for behavior. This is not a description of a research study. The school was provided with no external funding or extra person power. Ultimately, the school staff members were able to carry out the universal screening with relative ease with the resources they had available to them at the time. Although the application of the universal screening protocol followed research-based guidelines, the guidelines were adjusted to fit practical issues related to the school. In this way, this is an example of translating the research on universal screening to actual practice.

This description involves the implementation of a multiple-gating approach to universal screening in a large, ethnically diverse elementary school in Southern California serving 540 students. The school had an average class size of 29 students and 92 percent of the students were on free and reduced lunch. At the time school administrators sought consultation with the second author, the school only had a Tier I, schoolwide model of positive behavior support in place — there were no Tier II or III supports. The administrators were looking for a method of proactively identifying students in need of additional supports, since they did not know what to do with the group of students who were unresponsive to the universal tier of supports. The second author worked with school staff members to develop a universal screening protocol and create additional tiers of positive behavior support. A modified version of the SSBD was used as the universal screening procedure. The staff was trained on how to use the multiple-gating system during a three-hour in-service training. The universal screening protocol was implemented three months into the school year.

The first step consisted of using the teacher nomination form from the SSBD to have teachers rank order students who met profiles of externalizing and internalizing behavior patterns. Each teacher took an average of five minutes to rank order all the students in the class according to the behavior profiles (18 teachers X 5 minutes = 90 minutes total). The six students ranked at the top of the lists for the two behavior profiles from each class (three externalizing and three internalizing) were considered for additional support. This resulted in 112, or 20 percent, of all the students being passed on to the next step in the multiple-gating sequence. The next step involved teachers evaluating the 112 students' behaviors using two rating scales.

The Combined Frequency Index and Critical Events Index were distributed by the school team to the teachers. The teachers estimated that it took them roughly five minutes per student to complete the ratings, for a total of 30 minutes of time per teacher (18 teachers X 30 minutes = 540 minutes total). This is less than one, full preparation period for each teacher. The school team gathered the rating scales and scored them to determine which students exceeded normative cutoff points. It took team members an average of five minutes per student to score the two rating scales. Of the 112 students, 78 students exceeded normative cutoff points on at-least one of the rating scales. These 78 students passed through Gate 2 and were included in the next stage of assessment.

Typically, the SSBD has school staff members conduct direct observations of students' behavior on the playground and in the classroom. However, the school staff members believed that conducting direct observations of student behavior in multiple settings was beyond their staffing capabilities. Instead of conducting direct observations of student behavior on the playground and in the class, a team-based data review and selection process was used as Gate 3. There were six members of the school team (principal, school psychologist, school counselor, special educator, general educator, and paraeducator), and each member rank ordered the 78 students from most in need to least in need of additional positive behavior supports based on review of Gate 1 and 2 data. In light of the existing resources at the school, the school team determined that they could effectively accommodate 45 students (8 percent of all students) in the Tier II and III levels of positive behavior support. Students who were ranked in the top 45 on at least four of the six lists were automatically passed through Gate 3. Thirty-eight students were ranked within the top 45 on at least four of the six lists and, thus, selected for additional positive behavior supports. This left seven slots open for discussion. The school team selected the seven students with the highest ratings on the Combined Frequency Index and Critical Events Index for additional positive behavior supports. This stage of the assessment process was accomplished in an hour and half meeting held after school.

Within a week's time, the school was able to effectively implement the multiple-gating protocol and identify the top 8 percent of students who did not respond well to the universal tier of positive behavior supports. In total, the universal screening process took roughly 1700 minutes or 28 hours of educator time. This time, however, was distributed across 18 teachers and six school team members. Therefore, it took an average of 70 minutes or an hour and 10 minutes of time per educator to carry out the universal screening process. This indicates that educators used only an hour of prep time to complete the universal screening process, which is nickels and dimes compared to the benefits that will be seen by proactively identifying students at risk for developing an emotional and behavioral disorder and exposing them to more intensive positive behavior supports.

References

Artiles, A. J., & Trent, S. C. (1994). Overrepresentation of minority students in special education: A continuing debate. *The Journal of Special Education, 22*, 410-436.

Bullis, M., & Walker, H. M. (1994). *Comprehensive school-based systems for troubled youth*. Eugene, OR: University of Oregon, Center on Human Development.

Conroy, M. A., Hendrickson, J. M., & Hester, P. P. (2004). Early identification and prevention of emotional and behavioral disorders. In R. B. Rutherford, M. M. Quinn, & S. R. Mathur (Eds.), *Handbook of research in emotional and behavioral disorders* (pp. 199-215). New York: Guilford Press.

DiPerna, J. C., Volpe, R. J., & Elliott, S. N. (2002). A model of academic enablers and elementary reading/language arts achievement. *School Psychology Review, 31*, 298-312.

Drummond, T. (1993). *The Student Risk Screening Scale* (SRSS). Grants Pass, OR: Josephine County Mental Health Program.

Feil, E. G., Severson, H. H., & Walker, H. M. (2002). Early screening and intervention to prevent the development of aggressive, destructive behavior patterns among at-risk children. In M. R. Shinn, H. M. Walker, & G. Stoner (Eds.), *Interventions for academic and behavior problems II: Preventive and remedial approaches* (pp. 143–160). Bethesda, MD: National Association of School Psychologists.

Gerber, R., & Semmel, M. (1984). Teachers as imperfect tests: Reconceptualizing the referral process. *Educational Psychologist, 14*, 137-146.

Kauffman, J. M. (1999). How we prevent the prevention of emotional and behavioral disorders. *Exceptional Children, 65*(4), 448-468.

Kazdin, A. E. (1987). Treatment of antisocial behavior in children: Current status and future directions. *Psychological Bulletin, 102*, 187-203.

Lipsey, M. W., & Derzon, J. H. (1998). Predictors of violent or serious delinquency in adolescence and early adulthood: A synthesis of longitudinal research. In R. Loeber, & D. P. Farrington (Ed.), *Serious and violent juvenile offenders: Risk factors and successful interventions* (pp. 86-105). Thousand Oaks, CA: Sage Publications.

Lovitt (Eds). *Integrating general and special education* (pp. 23-48). Columbus, OH: Merrill/MacMillan.

Patterson, G. R., Reid, J. B., & Dishion, T. J. (1992). *Antisocial boys*. Eugene, OR: Castalia Press.

Smith, B. J., & Fox, L. (2003). *Systems of service delivery: A synthesis of evidence relevant to young children at-risk of or who have challenging behavior*. Denver, CO: Center for Evidence-based Practice: Young Children with Challenging Behavior.

Walker, H. M., & Severson, H. H. (1990). *Systematic screening for behavior disorders* (SSBD). Longmont, CO: Sopris West.

Walker, H. M., Ramsay, E., & Gresham, F. M. (2004). *Antisocial behavior in school: Evidence-based practices* (2d ed.). Belmont, CA: Wadsworth/Thomson Learning.

Zigler, E., Taussig, C., & Black, K. (1992). Early childhood intervention: A promising preventative for juvenile delinquency. *American Psychologist, 47*, 997-1006.

Chapter Three

Selecting Evidence-based Practices:
Building the Behavior 'Pyramid'

> After reading this chapter, you will be able to:
>
> ➤ describe the importance of adopting and implementing evidence-based approaches to reducing disruptive and antisocial behavior in schools;
>
> ➤ describe the definition and features of evidence-based behavior support practices; and
>
> ➤ build a behavior "pyramid" or menu of evidence-based behavior support interventions for your district or school.

The U.S. Department of Education provides a hierarchy of evidence-based (scientifically based) practices used to examine the level of research rigor applied to test an intervention. Increasingly, general and special education programs must provide evidence of using these evidence-based interventions. This chapter provides a framework for selecting and evaluating evidence-based interventions, and provides guidelines and examples of complying with legal requirements while allowing flexibility and control over intervention use.

Background

More and more children and youth are bringing well-developed patterns of antisocial and internalizing behavior to school. Our society's problems have spilled over into the process of schooling, so that ensuring school discipline and safety has emerged as a very high priority among parents of school-age children and youth. Classroom disruption, bullying, mean-spirited teasing, sexual harassment, and victimization are relatively commonplace occurrences on school campuses. In addition, the rate of juvenile crime for secondary students is higher on school campuses relative to the amount of time they spend there (Gottfredson, 2001). Nationally, secondary schools are the site of 37 percent of violent juvenile crimes; 81 percent of juvenile thefts, more than half of the youth carrying weapons; and 40 percent of fights. Of course you will need to continue responding reactively to these unacceptable events as they occur and minor sanctions will remain a part of your overall discipline plan. However, it is essential that you also begin investing in proactive, preventive approaches that will reduce their likely future occurrence, and function to restore offending students to the broader school community as much as possible.

Schools are faced with a number of challenges related to the growing population of disruptive, antisocial, and internalizing students:

- Disruptive students jeopardize the academic progress of other students, as well as their own.

- Internalizing students often go undetected, but are likely to experience a host of short- and long-term negative outcomes, such as drug and alcohol addiction; depression and school failure.

- Using sanctions, such as office referrals, suspensions and expulsions, are only a short-term fix to a chronic and long-term problem.

- The requirement to use evidence-based practices is confusing and creates financial and personal burdens on schools and school professionals.

Below we explore each of these challenges in detail, with an eye toward legally sound and practically feasible solutions.

Sanctions Alone Are Not a Solution

Removal from the classroom, commonly referred to as an office discipline referral (ODR) is used to remove disruptive or noncompliant students from classrooms or other settings, and to seek assistance in resolving the problem from a school administrator, or other designated school person. An ODR is not a true representation of "behavior," but rather it represents the protocol and definitions of behavior in a given school, the student's behavior, and the response of the teacher or other school adult. ODRs increasingly are being codified and tracked in electronic databases (see *www.swis.org*). Suspension and expulsion from school are methods used by school administrators to decrease violence, discourage drug abuse, and curtail criminal activities on campus. Suspension and expulsion also are used to deal with difficult and challenging behaviors, including truancy.

Punishing the at-risk student population and trying to exclude such students from schooling is not, by itself, an effective solution. Schools that use out-of-school suspension and expulsion without a comprehensive system of teaching, and rewards for expected behavior are shown to actually have higher rates of truancy, vandalism, and fighting (Mayer, 1995). Patterns of chronic suspension and expulsion have detrimental effects on teacher-student relations, gives the student reduced motivation to maintain self-control in school, does not teach alternative ways to behave, and has been shown in the research to have limited effects on long-term behavioral patterns. In fact, a history of chronic office referrals and suspension from school is a known risk factor for delinquency and school dropout. *This is not evidence-based practice!*

Programs and services need to be developed for students with challenging behaviors, and we need to do far better in developing strategies for including them in mainstream educational processes. A therapeutic and habilitative school posture must be adopted, whenever possible, in dealing with this student population, and ways of supporting and reclaiming them must be selected and implemented faithfully. Longitudinal research shows that school engagement, bonding, and success serve as powerful protective factors in adolescence, buffering students from a number of destructive outcomes including violent delinquent acts, heavy drinking, teenage sex, and school dropout (Hawkins, Catalano, Kosterman, Abbott, & Hill, 1999).

School Practices Can Make the Problem Worse

Many school practices may unintentionally contribute to the development of emotional and behavior problems and academic failure. For example, the overemphasis on detecting and changing individual child or youth characteristics that predict learning problems or disruption may cause schools to overlook many important variables (Gresham, 1991). Researchers have labeled this endeavor the search for "within" child pathology. The important variables that are often overlooked include, among others:

1. Ineffective instruction that results in academic failure;

2. Reactive versus systematic and planful early and chronic screening for academic and behavioral adjustment problems (see Chapter 2);

3. Failure to individualize instruction and support to adapt to individual differences (e.g., ethnic and cultural differences, gender, disability);

4. Failure to assist students from at-risk (e.g., poverty, racial/ethnic minority members) backgrounds to bond with and engage in the schooling process;

5. Inconsistent and punitive classroom and behavior management practices;

6. Lack of opportunity to learn and practice prosocial interpersonal and self-management skills;

7. Unclear rules and expectations regarding appropriate behavior;

8. Failure to effectively correct rule violations and reward adherence to them;

9. Disagreement and inconsistency of implementation among staff members; and

10. Lack of meaningful administrator involvement, leadership, and support.

Neglecting these school practices could lead to harmful outcomes for students. Thankfully, they are all amenable to change by using scientifically designed and delivered staff development methods, and by adopting and implementing evidence-based best practices. Schools are the ideal setting to organize efforts against the increasing problems of at-risk children and youth (Walker et al., 1996). Unfortunately, school personnel have a long history of focusing solutions elsewhere or of applying simple and unproven solutions to complex behavior problems (e.g., office discipline referrals, suspensions, expulsions, restraints, seclusion, referral to special education). They express understandable disappointment when these strategies do not work as expected. Moreover, these ineffective practices may provide short-term relief for schools by eliminating the presenting problem for a brief period of time (i.e., remove the student via suspension or to self-contained special education classes), but their long-term effects often include failure to focus on the administrative, teaching and management practices that either contribute to, or reduce school violence (Tobin & Sugai, 1999). Interventions must be implemented that integrate whole school and individual approaches.

Educators in today's schools and classrooms must adopt and sustain effective, evidence-based and cost-efficient practices (Gottfredson et al., 2000). Evidence-based approaches to effective schoolwide discipline and academic support, for example, include: (a) systematic social skills instruction; (b) academic and curricular restructuring; (c) positive, behaviorally based interventions; (d) early screening and identification of students with behavior problems and learning difficulties; (e) positive schoolwide discipline systems; (f) and timely and effective instruction (Biglan, 1995; Mayer, 1995; Sprague, Sugai, & Walker, 1998; Sugai, Horner, & Gresham, 2002).

Policy and practice generally lag well behind the research that validates evidence-based approaches that can inform and guide regulations and practices based upon them. This is especially true in the area of school discipline and prevention of emotional and behavior problems. The pressures and demands of the moment force us into making decisions about school discipline practices that may appear promising but may not, as yet, be proven through the research process. Thus, we are left with basing many of our decisions upon practices that appear promising; relying on our experience and using our best judgment, until the knowledge base on school evidence-based practices becomes more solid, cohesive, evidence-based and widely used.

What Is 'Evidence-based' or 'Scientifically Based'?

Evidence-based practices are used in two ways: (1) for selecting interventions, and (2) for evaluating the effectiveness of the intervention and the degree of fidelity with which it is applied (essentially, is it being used as it was designed to be used; is it being done right?). This sets the stage for the necessary shift in schools from "paper implementation" to "process implementation" involving high-quality supports and clear evidence that students are learning or their behavior is changing (Fixsen, Naoom, Blase, Friedman, & Wallace, 2005).

The U.S. Department of Education provides hierarchy of "scientifically based" practices based on the level of research rigor applied to test an intervention. At the highest level of rigor is a randomized controlled trial design (random selection or assignment to a condition), followed by a quasi-experimental controlled design (typically denotes non-random assignment to condition). Opinions of respected authorities also are listed. Additional evidence of efficacy is indicated by studies with a statistically significant positive effect; a positive effect sustained for at least one year post-intervention; and replication of the effect in one or more settings, and/or populations. Table 1 illustrates the hierarchy and defines the key features of each level of evidence. You also should see the No Child Left Behind Act to review the legal requirements for using evidence-based interventions and supports: *www.ed.gov/nclb/landing.jhtml?src=pb*.

Table 1

Levels of Evidence for Efficacy and Effectiveness

Criterion	I-A	I-B	II-A	II-B	III	IV
Randomized controlled trial design	•					
Quasi-experimental controlled design		•	•	•		
Statistically significant positive effect	•	•	•	•	•	
Positive effect sustained for at least one year post-intervention	•	•		•		
Positive effect replicated in one or more settings and/or populations	•	•	•		•	
Opinions of respected authorities						•

Level I-A: The effectiveness of the program has been established in at least one study using an experimental design in which a sufficient number of subjects have been randomly assigned to either an intervention or a control group. In addition, the outcome of the program shows a statistically significant positive effect, and the effect is sustained for at least one year post-intervention. Evidence is stronger if the beneficial effect has been replicated in one or more settings.

Level I-B: Evidence obtained from at least one well-designed quasi-experimental controlled trial without randomization, in which a sufficient number of subjects have been assigned to either an intervention or a comparison group. As in the case of Level I-A, the outcome of the program shows a statistically significant positive effect, the effect is sustained for at least one year post-intervention, and the evidence is stronger if the beneficial effect has been replicated in one or more settings.

Level II-A: Evidence obtained using an experimental or quasi-experimental design, the outcome shows a significant positive effect, and the beneficial effect has been replicated in at least one setting.

Level II-B: Evidence obtained using an experimental or quasi-experimental design, the outcome shows a significant positive effect, and the beneficial effect has been sustained for at least one year.

Level III: Evidence obtained over time from strong and replicated results in studies with no control group.

Level IV: Opinions of respected authorities, based on clinical experience, descriptive studies, or reports of expert committees.

What the Science Says about What Does and Does Not Work in Schools

Evidence-based best practice for supporting students with challenging behavior begins with identifying problems early, whether the problems are academic, emotional, behavioral, or interpersonal (Sprague & Nishioka, 2003/2004; Sprague & Walker, 2005; Tobin & Sprague, 2003). After identification, interventions become essential to addressing the problem directly and thus reducing obstacles to successful school adjustment. If appropriate educational and behavioral supports were more widely provided, the long-term benefits would greatly exceed the costs.

Researchers in the area of school discipline, substance abuse prevention, and delinquency prevention effectiveness have identified a range of evidence-based strategies that result in positive outcomes for children and youth with emotional and behavioral problems, as well as those strategies and approaches that either do not work or actually make things worse. These researchers have studied national samples of schools to identify the factors, conditions and characteristics that make them safer and more effective (Gottfredson, 2001; Greenberg, Domitrovich, & Bumbarger, 1999; Tobin & Sprague, 2003; Tolan & Guerra, 1994). Their work is highly recommended as a trustworthy and reliable source of information on this topic. Table 2, next page, lists generic strategies recommended as effective and those that are considered to be ineffective. Table 3, page 41, lists recommended Web sites providing reviews of intervention effectiveness.

Table 2

Typology of Evidence-based Intervention Strategies

Adult-Focused Interventions	Student-Focused Interventions
What Works or Is Promising	
<ul><li>Programs aimed at building school capacity to initiate and sustain innovation</li><li>Sustained workshop and staff development opportunities</li><li>Follow up consultation and assistance</li><li>Altering school policies</li><li>Administrator involvement (required)</li><li>Informing and involving families</li><li>Data-based decision-making and regular feedback to implementers</li><li>Using published or standardized curriculum materials</li><li>Active and positive supervision in common areas (adult proximity and presence to prevent problem behavior and interfere with deviant peer affiliation)</li><li>Altering ecological arrangements</li><li>Positive reinforcement for displaying expected behavior (e.g., staff meeting recognition, other non-monetary rewards)</li><li>Time for planning and communication among implementers (collegial relations among adults)</li><li>Programs that improve classroom management and that use effective instructional techniques.</li><li>Basing individual behavior support plans on Functional Behavioral Assessment results</li></ul>	<ul><li>Programs aimed at clarifying and communicating norms about behaviors by establishing school rules, improving the consistency of their enforcement (particularly when they emphasize positive reinforcement of appropriate behavior), or communicating norms through schoolwide campaigns (e.g., anti-bullying campaigns) or ceremonies</li><li>Teaching positive behavioral expectations</li><li>Activities to promote rule clarity and acceptance</li><li>Positive reinforcement for displaying expected behavior (e.g., token economies, verbal praise)</li><li>Correcting inappropriate behavior and prompting expected behavior</li><li>"Booster" reminders of expected behavior (posted signs, assemblies, school announcements, T-shirts)</li><li>4:1 positive to negative interactions between adults and children</li><li>Collegial relations among adults and students</li><li>Comprehensive instructional programs that teach a range of social competency skills (e.g., developing self-control, stress-management, responsible decision-making, social problem-solving, and communication skills) and that are delivered over a long period of time to continually reinforce skills</li></ul>
What Does NOT Work	
<ul><li>Episodic, "one-shot" workshops with no follow-up coaching</li><li>Not sharing performance-based data with implementers</li></ul>	<ul><li>Counseling students, particularly in a peer-group context</li><li>Offering youths alternative activities, such as recreation and community service activities, in the absence of more potent prevention programming</li><li>Instructional programs focusing on information dissemination fear arousal, moral appeal, and affective education (e.g., just say "no")</li></ul>

Table 3

Recommended Web-sites for Selecting and Evaluating Evidence-based Practices
2002 Surgeon General's Report on Antisocial Behavior (*http://www.surgeongeneral.gov/library/youthviolence/*)
Center on Social and Emotional Foundations for Early Learning (*http://www.csefel.uiuc.edu/what-works.html*)
Florida PBS Project (*http://flpbs.fmhi.usf.edu/index.asp*)
Center for the Study and Prevention of Violence (*http://www.colorado.edu/cspv/*)
Safe and Responsive Schools Project (*http://www.indiana.edu/~safeschl/index.html*)
Collaborative for Academic, Social and Emotional Learning (*http://www.casel.org/home/index.php*)

Issues to Consider in Selecting Evidence-based Practices

While many programs have been shown to be effective in research studies, much less is known about what it takes to get them implemented well in typical schools (Fixsen, Naoom, Blase, Friedman, & Wallace, 2005). There are several important questions to ask while selecting and designing behavioral interventions:

- **Is there evidence of effectiveness?** When looking at the research, it's important to ask if typical educators are capable of implementing the intervention effectively, or if the researchers got the effect only when they ran it.

- **How much does the intervention cost?** Interventions that are excessively costly are not likely to be used, or even tried. There also may be expensive, ongoing requirements to work with the developers of the program. Educators and administrators will want to carefully investigate the possibility of any hidden cost.

- **How big an effect should I expect?** Many evidence-based practices are considered effective even if the improvements are small. As such, it's important to ask if the practice is shown to have a large or small effect. Often with behavioral supports, changes are slow and small; unless they understand this and keep focused on the data, your staff members can become frustrated with the results or the extra efforts required to carry out the intervention. It is important to keep in mind that the "silver bullet" intervention does not exist. That means some interventions will work better than others for particular students.

- **Is there evidence of effectiveness (did typical people guide the intervention?) vs., efficacy (did the researchers get the effect only when they ran it?)?** It is typical to conduct research studies guided by the developers (and often implemented by them) in order to demonstrate that an intervention can work. Once there is evidence of effectiveness, it is important to test the intervention in "real world" application in schools. The general finding is that adherence to the program will be lower in typical settings, and that the results obtained in the effectiveness trial will not be as dramatic. You should carefully consider this when selecting an evidence-based intervention.

- **Can teachers integrate the intervention into their daily routine?** This may be the most important question of all. Many educators are reluctant to adopt behavior support practices that do not fit with the daily life of our classrooms. We have been influenced by work on social marketing — a media-related approach to dissemination of science-based practice that attempts to "sell" behavior changes (Wallack, 1990). Social marketing principles, in which marketing concepts are integrated with social influence practices, have successfully guided the health field in its attempts to improve individuals' health behaviors. These principles underscore the importance of making it as easy and attractive as possible for the consumer (your staff members) to understand and value the messages of adopting evidence-based practices, through mix of the "four Ps": (1) product (what is the proposed intervention); (2) price (what is the personal or social cost of using the new practice); (3) promotion (what are the benefits for my students, for me?); and (4) place (availability of the intervention — where can I see it in action?). In light of the importance of quick observable results that provide immediate reinforcement, social marketing approaches have been successfully used to promote adoption of behavioral innovations in schools (Embry, in press).

Building the Behavior Pyramid at the Universal, Selective, and Tertiary Levels

In Chapter 1 you were introduced to the three-tiered prevention model. This model forms the backbone of an effective RTI approach that aims to match the intensity of student need with the type and intensity of intervention or support.

Schools have always been judged by how well their students perform academically. While destructive or violent behavior is a top concern and a direct influence on academic performance, systematic approaches to assessing schools on the basis of behavioral success or failure are not currently well developed. However, our schools are experiencing a strong push toward accountability on just that front.

Parents, schools, and community leaders need to make informed judgments about which systems are in place to prevent school violence and later emotional and behavioral disorders. Title IV of the No Child Left Behind (NCLB) Act requires public schools to focus on the critical role of comprehensive needs assessment information in building and maintaining a school environment that is safe and conducive to learning.

In order to receive funds under Title IV, Part A, schools must adhere to the NCLB Principles of Effectiveness as follows:

- Assess the specific safety risk and protective influences on the school;

- Establish measurable goals and objectives for improvement that are based on those identified needs;

- Base projected changes on appropriate measurements; and,

- Use evidence-based interventions for effecting improvement.

School safety and prevention plans must target what is required for the school to become safer and describe the activities or programs to be adopted that will address those targets. These activities and programs must show research evidence of effectiveness in improving school safety, involve parents in the assessment process, and include performance measures to gauge effectiveness. In addition, each school district must have a comprehensive plan for school safety that includes policies, security procedures, prevention activities, crisis response procedures, and a code of conduct for students that incorporates a "wrong and harmful" message about illegal drug use and violence. The plan needs to be made available to the public for review and comment.

Because of the importance of gathering and maintaining consistent data that provide a picture of how a school is performing, the new law requires school districts to monitor and report truancy rates, suspensions and expulsions related to drugs and violence, the incidence, prevalence, and age of onset of alcohol use, drug use, and violence by youths (youth also are asked about perceptions of health risks, and social disapproval for use) and, incidents of criminal activity on school property.

Positive Behavior Supports: The Foundation of the Pyramid

There is growing evidence that a program-wide, systems approach to behavior management can prevent many of the problems that school settings often exacerbate (Metzler, Biglan et al., 2001; Metzler, Biglan, Rusby, & Sprague, 2001; Sprague et al., 2002; Taylor-Greene et al., 1997). Commonly referred to as Positive Behavior Support (PBS), PBS is a multiple-systems approach to addressing the problems posed by students with emotional and behavior problems and coping with challenging forms of student behavior. The key practices of PBS include: (a) clear definitions of expected appropriate, positive behaviors provided for students and staff members; (b) clear definitions of problem behaviors and their consequences for students and staff members; (c) regularly scheduled instruction in desired positive social behaviors to enable students to acquire the necessary skills for the desired behavior change; (d) effective incentives and motivational systems provided to encourage students to behave appropriately; (e) school staff committed to staying with the intervention over the long term to monitor, support, coach, debrief, and provide booster lessons for students as necessary to maintain the achieved gains; (f) staff who receive training, feedback, and coaching about effective implementation of the intervention; and (g) established systems for measuring and monitoring the intervention's effectiveness that are carried out regularly.

These practices are highly likely to ensure that positive behavior is supported in all settings, and they continuously monitor student behavior patterns at the individual and group level. A series of studies (Metzler et al., 2001; Reid, Eddy, Fetrow, & Stoolmiller, 1999; Sprague et al., 2002) has documented the effects of PBS interventions. Studies have shown dramatic reductions in office discipline referrals (up to 50 percent), with continued improvement over a three-year period in schools that sustain the PBS intervention (Irvin, Tobin, Sprague, Sugai, & Vincent, 2004). Comparison schools consistently show increases or no change in office referrals, along with general frustration with the existing school discipline program(s). In addition, school staff members report greater satisfaction with work, compared to staff in schools without PBS.

In studies employing the components included in PBS interventions, reductions in antisocial behavior (Sprague et al., 2002), vandalism (Mayer, 1995), aggression (Grossman et al., 1997; Lewis, Colvin, & Sugai, 2000), later delinquency (Kellam, 1998), and alcohol, tobacco, and other drug use (O'Donnell, Hawkins, Catalano, Abbott, & Day, 1995) have been documented. Positive changes in protective factors, such as academic achievement (Kellam et al., 1998; O'Donnell et al., 1997) and school engagement (O'Donnell et al., 1997) have been documented using a positive school discipline program in concert with other prevention interventions.

Over 6000 U.S. schools have adopted and are implementing schoolwide PBS interventions, and hundreds more have been exposed to the practices through statewide workshops, institutes, and conferences. There is a need to effectively scale up this foundational response to preventing emotional and behavioral problems. There are recent data that indicate when a schoolwide PBS system is implemented conjointly with an evidence-based, universal academic system, 95 percent of the student population is likely to respond effectively to the universal tier of supports (McIntosh, Chard, Boland, & Horner, 2006).

43

What Works with At-risk and High-risk Youth? The Top Tiers

Many at-risk students leave school without a diploma and are ill-prepared to function as a productive adult. In addition to the problem of school dropouts, students who experience academic difficulties are at risk for becoming involved in juvenile crime (Reid, Patterson, & Snyder, 2002) and for behavior problems at school.

At-risk students often come to school with emotional and behavioral difficulties that interfere with their attempts to focus on academic instruction. Others may have interpersonal issues with other students or school staff members that make concentrating on learning difficult. Best practice for these students begins with early identification of emotional, behavioral, and interpersonal needs, followed by interventions to reduce obstacles to successful school adjustment.

Walker et al., (1996) recommend that every school provide a foundation for at-risk student supports by building a schoolwide positive behavior support system. This foundation should always include schoolwide PBS (Sprague & Golly, 2004; Sugai & Horner, 2002) and other studies also support the use of schoolwide curricula that teach anger management, impulse control, thinking skills, and problem-solving (see *www.casel.org* for an excellent review of the effectiveness and usability of these curricula).

Effective interventions for at-risk and high-risk students include: (a) school-based services, (b) family support services, and (c) service coordination services. The following paragraphs provide a brief overview. Figure 2, below, provides a sample "menu" of interventions at Tiers I, II and III.

Figure 2

An Example of Three Tiers of Intervention for Behavioral RTI

Tier I Basics — This forms the base available for all students, in every classroom, and throughout the school campus.

- **Unconditional positive regard** shown for each student, by all, regardless of challenging behavior.

- **4 to 1 positive gestures and comments** to corrective statements are given for each student.

- **Human needs are fostered** in each class, through teacher-designed interactions.

    - Fun

    - Freedom

    - Empowerment

    - Belonging

- **Individual and group reinforcement** is available, with choices given within whole group design.

- **On-going rule & procedure teaching** and **reinforcement** occurs: Safe, Respectful, Responsible.

- **Differentiated instruction and accommodations** for student characteristics are given.

Tier II Basics — These interventions are implemented based on a systematic procedure that identifies students who are non-responsive to Tier I.

- **Daily report cards** with reinforcement for increasing behavioral success.

- **Mentoring programs** (one on one regularly occurring sessions with an identified staff person who befriends and supports).

- **Check-in/Check-out systems** (Student meets with a staff person to review target behavior and receive encouragement and self-monitoring data sheet in a.m., and reviews results in p.m.)

- **Self-monitoring systems** (Student records success/failure in specific time intervals in classes.)

- **Behavior contracting** (Student, staff, family agree on specific outcomes for specific behaviors.)

- **Social skills instruction or school counseling** (Student participates in on-going school sessions.)

Tier III Basics — These interventions are highly individualized and selected and implemented based on non-responsiveness to Tier II coupled with the presenting need determined by the team.

- **Function-based behavior planning process** (Student receives a functional behavioral assessment, with a behavior plan developed based on that assessment. The plan addresses three pathways: 1. Supporting desired positive behaviors; 2. Reacting skillfully and safely to problem behavior; 3. Teaching and reinforcing functionally equivalent replacement behavior, and acceptable alternative.)

- **Family therapy** (Needs-based referrals and communication systems are provided.)

- **Multi-systemic wrap around services** (Implemented when the severity warrants this service.)

- **Cognitive behavioral therapy** (CBT is implemented by school staff or referrals, when student's faulty reasoning and emotional response to neutral stimuli warrants addressing these underlying barriers to academic and behavioral success.)

School-based Supports for Students and Families

Although we recommend tailoring services to meet the needs of individual students, we suggest employing a general framework of evidence-based interventions in the school. These supports include school-based adult mentoring, individualized social skills training, increased academic support, self-monitoring, and alternatives to out-of-school suspension and expulsion, and school-based service coordination.

Adult Mentorship

A critical goal of supports is to build a connection between the student and the school. To accomplish this, staff members and other adults in the school served as mentors (Hawken & Horner, 2003). The mentor meets daily with his or her assigned students to foster a positive mentoring relationship. The mentor coaches the student to make positive behavior changes in school, monitors the student's behavior and academic performance in school, and, most importantly, provides the presence of a trusted adult at school. Examples of mentor-based support systems include: Check and Connect (Sinclair, Christenson, Evelo, & Hurley, 1998) and the Behavior Education Program (Crone, Horner, & Hawken, 2004).

Social Skills Training

If children and youth have unsatisfactory teacher-related or peer-related social skills relatively early in their school careers, they are at increased risk for later school failure. In fact, researchers have clearly documented associations between the success and failure of teacher-and peer-related adjustments and a variety of long-term adaptive and maladaptive outcomes (Coie, Dodge, & Kupersmidt, 1990; Parker & Asher, 1987; Crews, Bender, Gresham, Vanderwood, & Cook, 2006). Learning social skills also has implications for academic performance. In a major longitudinal study, Caprara and colleagues found that social skills of third-graders, as assessed by teachers, were better predictors of eighth-grade academic achievement than achievement tests results in third grade (Caprara, Barbarnelli, Pastorelli, Bandura, & Zimbardo, 2000).

Social skills training has been established as an evidence-based intervention for students with or at risk for emotional and behavioral disorders (Cook, Gresham, Kern, Barreras, Thornton, & Crews, 2008; Gresham, Cook, Kern, & Crews, 2005). Several social skills curricula have been developed that cover a variety of topics, such as appropriately asking for help and permission, initiating and maintaining conversations, initiating a play activity, sharing belongings, expressing frustration, establishing friendships, responding to peer pressure, sportsmanship, following instructions, and a host of other important social skills. Social skills lessons incorporate a variety of strategies including: describing or modeling the behavior to be learned; role playing to allow the student the chance to demonstrate and practice the behavior while receiving feedback; and homework to facilitate the use of the newly acquired skills in other settings. Individualized social skills training is an intensive intervention that requires pulling the student out of class. All students who do not respond well to the Tier I supports do not need individualized social skills training, because it is an intensive intervention that requires students to be pulled out of class and miss valuable instructional time. In our experience, individualized social skills training fits best within the Tier III level of supports. The following are social skills curricula that can be purchased for use in your schools:

- The Social Skills Improvement System developed by Elliott and Gresham (2008)

- The Walker Social Skills Program developed by Hill Walker

- Skill-Streaming developed by Arnold Goldstein

- Teaching Social Skills to Youth published by *Boys Town Press*

- Stop and Think Social Skills Program developed by Howard Knoff

Academic Supports

School-based supports should include specialized academic and social skills instruction using multiple strategies to meet individual student needs. An important feature of the supports should include: classroom environments structured to provide positive vs. punishing behavior management; low student-to-teacher ratios; and research-based teaching strategies providing individual and small group instruction for the at-risk students. The curriculum areas addressed within the alternative classroom setting may include functional life skills necessary for successful transition to responsible adult living (e.g., vocational, self-management, leisure, and independent living skills) (Bullis, Nishioka-Evans, Fredericks, & Davis, 1993). Furthermore, staff members may conduct intensive social skills training to include interpersonal communication, problem-solving, coping with feelings, and making friends in small group settings that include selected typical peers to enhance skill building and reduce stigmatization, and the potential for deviancy training (Dishion, Eddy, Haas, Li, & Spracklen, 1997).

Individualized academic supports can be provided in regular classroom settings, tutorial help with regular classroom assignments, basic skill instruction, and study skills training. Support services in the regular classroom allow teachers to identify specific skills and strategies that the student could use to promote positive relationships with the teacher and other students (Walker, Hops, & Greenwood, 1988).

Self-Monitoring

Many have argued that the ultimate goal of education is to develop self-determined individuals. Field, Martin, Miller, Ward, and Wehmeyer (1998) defined self-determination as a combination of skills, knowledge, and beliefs that enable a person to engage in goal-directed, self-regulated, autonomous behavior. Students at risk for developing an emotional and behavioral disorder have significant deficits in self-determination (Benetiz, Lattimore, & Wehmeyer, 2007). Self-monitoring is an evidence-based intervention that supports at-risk students in the development of self-determined behavior. Self-monitoring interventions make students aware of their own behavior by monitoring it at preset or random time points throughout the school day. For example, students can keep track of and record the number of minutes they remain on-task during a specific period in which they are likely to engage in off-task, disruptive behavior. Teachers tend to love self-monitoring interventions because it requires little time to implement, and students are held accountable for monitoring and tracking their own behavior. Self-monitoring is an excellent intervention to use for students involved in the Tier II or Tier III levels of positive behavior support. Figure 3, next page, illustrates a sample self-monitoring form.

Figure 3

Sample Self-Monitoring Form

Daily Self Monitoring Chart

Student Name:_____   Date:_____

Target Behaviors	Period 1		Period 2		Period 3		Period 4	
	Time 1	Time 2	Time 1	Time 2	Time 1	Time 2	Time 1	Time 2
	Yes No	Yes No	Yes No	Yes No	Yes No	Yes No	Yes No	Yes No
Raised hand to ask question or get out of seat	— —	— —	— —	— —	— —	— —	— —	— —
Kept hands and feet to self	— —	— —	— —	— —	— —	— —	— —	— —
Worked on class assignments	— —	— —	— —	— —	— —	— —	— —	— —
Followed teacher instructions	— —	— —	— —	— —	— —	— —	— —	— —
Totals	— —	— —	— —	— —	— —	— —	— —	— —

Goal (number of total "yes" to "no"):_____

Alternative Discipline, Including Alternatives to Out-of-School Suspension

Alternative discipline supports may include a point and level system (Walker, 1995; Walker, 1997), frequent positive rewards, and individualized behavior interventions that support the practice of positive social skills in regular school settings. If necessary, staff members will conduct a functional behavioral assessment (see Chapters 4 and 7) to develop individualized behavior support plans. Consequently, student behavior support plans must consider the function of — or reason why — the student used the problem behavior, taught appropriate replacement skills for socially unacceptable behavior and taught self-management skills (O'Neill et al., 1997).

Between 79 percent and 94 percent of schools have policies known as "zero tolerance" — the term given to a school or district policy that mandates predetermined consequences for various student offenses — and almost 90 percent of Americans support these policies. However, out-of-school suspension and expulsion can, at best, be considered a stop-gap measure, not intervention (Johns, Carr, & Hoots, 1997; Skiba, 2000)! It is critically important to consider potential physical health, mental health, and safety concerns that arise from suspension and expulsion from school. Your school system should provide, through its own system and through community partnerships, an environment and a range of resources that support students and that decrease the likelihood that students will engage in behaviors requiring disciplinary action (American Academy of Pediatrics Committee on School Health, 2003). Suggested alternatives to these practices include: supervised suspension rooms (in-school suspension), alternative education, parent accompanies student to school, and community service or service learning (Johns et al., 1997).

Family Support

A few students will need more comprehensive services to support their success in school and the community. The families of these students often have difficulty providing the supervision and stability required to adequately support their child in school. Moreover, the chronic patterns of adverse life events they experienced on a daily basis often make school attendance and academic success a low priority (Patterson, 1982). Given this, a primary goal of family support should be to build collaborative partnerships between the student's family and the school to increase parental school involvement (Hawkins et al., 1999). Staff members should work collaboratively with parents to build school/home interventions that increase positive relationships, limit setting, monitoring, praise, and constructive problem-solving — factors that reduce the likelihood of school and community failure for at-risk students (Reid et al., 2002).

School-home notes are an evidence-based intervention that has been shown to effectively reduce student problem behavior and enlist parental involvement and support in the educational service delivery process. School-home notes require parents and teachers to join efforts in establishing expectations for social behavior performance at school, teachers to rate students on any number of target behaviors, and parents to provide consequences based on the evaluation. When implemented correctly, this is a powerful intervention, because students are able to learn that behavior at school determines whether they have access to privileges or earn predetermined rewards. School-home notes fit nicely within Tier II of positive behavior supports because they require little assessment and are relatively easy to develop and implement. Figure 4, next page, is an example school-home note.

Figure 4

A⁺ _____   **School-Home Note**

| Name: _____ | Date: _____ |

	Classroom					
	Before Lunch			After Lunch		
Behaviors	Needs Work	Okay	Excellent	Needs Work	Okay	Excellent
Respected other students						
Worked on class assignments						
Followed Teacher Instructions						
Target Behavior:						

	On the Yard					
	Morning Recess			Afternoon Recess		
Behaviors	Needs Work	Okay	Excellent	Needs Work	Okay	Excellent
Interacted well with others						
Yard rules						
Target Behavior:						

Teacher comments: _____

_____

Teacher Signature:_____

Describe how you responded to your child's performance today (e.g., praised child, earned activity, loss of privilege, extra chore): _____

_____

Comment for teacher:

_____

Parent Signature:_____

Service Coordination

For some students, staff members will need to match community services to individual student and family needs. Best educational practice suggests developing a program support plan with the student, their parents, and involved community agency representatives (Eber, 2003). The purpose of this plan is to organize systematic and integrated services across school, home, and community settings that will assist students in reducing anti-social behavior and increase positive school engagement. The purpose of service coordination is to build linkages to community agencies that ensure selected students have a stable adult-mentoring relationship, shelter, food, safety, and medical care. Moreover, staff members may work collaboratively with community agencies to increase after-school supervision, encourage activities with non-delinquent peers, and build mental health support for students in managing the many stressful events of their day-to-day life.

Building Your Three-tiered Menu of Supports

Figure 5, next page, provides a worksheet for you to complete to build and assess the adequacy and comprehensiveness of a three-tiered menu of support strategies at your school. We recommend that you start by listing all of the interventions you know, and also consider how students are selected to receive those supports. While Tier I or universal supports are provided to all students regardless of their risk status, it becomes critical to carefully consider how students are selected for Tier II and III supports. (Chapters 2 and 4 describe how to make data-based decisions within an RTI model for behavior to identify students for Tier II and Tier III supports.)

Figure 5

RTI and Behavior Planning Menu

Intervention Intensity	Intervention	How are students selected to receive this intervention?
Targeted/Intensive (Few)		
Selected (Some)		
Universal (All)		

References

Biglan, A. (1995). Translating what we know about the context of antisocial behavior into a lower prevalence of such behavior. *Journal of Applied Behavior Analysis, 28*(4), 479-492.

Bullis, M., Nishioka-Evans, V., Fredericks, H. D. B., & Davis, C. (1993). Identifying and assessing the job-related social skills of adolescents and young adults with emotional and behavioral disorders. *Journal of Emotional and Behavioral Disorders, 1*(4), 216-250.

Dishion, T. J., Eddy, M., Haas, E., Li, F., & Spracklen, K. (1997). Friendships and violent behavior during adolescence. *Social Development, 6*, 207-223.

Eber, L. (2003). *The art & science of wraparound: Completing the continuum of school wide behavioral support* (Instruction manual ed.): Indiana University.

Fixsen, D. L., Naoom, S. F., Blase, K. A., Friedman, R. M., & Wallace, F. (2005). *Implementation Research: A Synthesis of the Literature*. Tampa, FL: University of South Florida, Louis de la Parte Florida Mental Health Institute, The National Implementation Research Network (FMHI Publication #231).

Fixsen, G., Naoom, S. F., Blase, K. A., Friedman, R. M., & Wallace, F. (2005). *Implementation Research: A Synthesis of the Literature*. Tampa, FL: University of South Florida, Louis de la Parte Florida Mental Health Institute, The National Implementation Research Network (FMHI Publication #231).

Gottfredson, G. D. (2001). *Delinquency in schools*. New York: Cambridge University Press.

Gottfredson, G. D., Gottfredson, D. C., Czeh, E. R., Cantor, D., Crosse, S. B., & Hantman, I. (2000). *National study of deliquency prevention in schools*. Ellicott City, MD: Gottfredson Associates.

Greenberg, M. T., Domitrovich, C., & Bumbarger, B. (1999). *Preventing mental disorders in school-age children: A review of the effectiveness of prevention programs*. Submitted to: Center for Mental Health Services, Substance Abuse Mental Health Services Administration, and U.S. Department of Health and Human Services.

Gresham, F. (1991). Conceptualizing behavior disorders in terms of resistance to intervention. *School Psychology Review, 20*, 23-36.

Grossman, D. C., Neckerman, H. J., Koepsell, T. D., Liu, P.-Y., Asher, K. N., & Beland, K., et al. (1997). Effectiveness of a violence prevention curriculum among children in elementary school: A randomized controlled trial. *Journal of the American Medical Association, 277*(20), 1605-1611.

Hawken, L. C., & Horner, R. H. (2003). Evaluation of a targeted group intervention within a school-wide system of behavior support. *Journal of Behavioral Education, 12*(3), 225-240.

Hawkins, J. D., Catalano, R. F., Kosterman, R., Abbott, R., & Hill, K. G. (1999). Preventing adolescent health-risk behaviors by strengthening protection during childhood. *Archives of Pediatrics & Adolescent Medicine, 153*, 226-234.

Irvin, L. K., Tobin, T. J., Sprague, J. R., Sugai, G., & Vincent, C. G. (2004). Validity of office discipline referral measures as indices of school-wide behavioral status and effects of school-wide behavioral interventions. *Journal of Positive Behavior Interventions, 6*(3), 131-147.

Johns, B. H., Carr, V. G., & Hoots, C. W. (1997). *Reduction of school violence: Alternatives to suspension* (Second ed.). Horsham, PA: LRP Publications.

Kellam, S. G., Mayer, L. S., Rebok, G. W., & Hawkins, W. E. (1998). Effects of improving achievement on aggressive behavior and of improving aggressive behavior on achievement through two preventive interventions: An investigation of causal paths. In B. P. Dohrenwend (Ed.), *Adversity, stress, and psychopathology* (pp. 486-505, 567). New York: Oxford University Press.

Lewis, T. J., Colvin, G., & Sugai, G. (2000). The effects of precorrection and active supervision on the recess behavior of elementary school students. *School Psychology Quarterly, 23*(2), 109-121.

Mayer, G. R. (1995). Preventing antisocial behavior in the schools. *Journal of Applied Behavior Analysis, 28*(4), 467-478.

McIntosh, K., Chard, D. J., Boland, J. B., & Horner, R. H. (2006). Demonstration of combined efforts in school-wide academic and behavioural systems and incidence of reading and behaviour challenges in early elementary grades. *Journal of Positive Behaviour Interventions, 8*, 146-154.

Metzler, C. W., Biglan, A., Rusby, J. C., & Sprague, J. R. (2001). Evaluation of a comprehensive behavior management program to improve school wide positive behavior support. *Education and Treatment of Children, 24*(4), 448-479.

O'Donnell, J., Hawkins, J., Catalano, R., Abbott, R., & Day, L. (1995). Preventing school failure, drug use, and delinquency among low-income children: long-term intervention in elementary schools. *American Journal of Orthopsychiaty, 65*, 87-100.

O'Neill, R. E., Horner, R. H., Albin, R. W., Sprague, J. R., Newton, S., & Storey, K. (1997). *Functional assessment and program development for problem behavior: A practical handbook.* (Second ed.). Pacific Grove, CA: Brookes/Cole Publishing.

Patterson, G. R. (1982). *Coercive family process.* Eugene, OR: Castalia.

Reid, J., Eddy, M., Fetrow, R., & Stoolmiller, M. (1999). Description and immediate impacts of a preventative intervention for conduct problems. *American Journal of Community Psychology, 24*(4), 483-517.

Reid, J., Patterson, G., & Snyder, J. (2002). *Antisocial behavior in children and adolescents: A developmental analysis and model for intervention.* Washington, DC: American Psychological Association.

Sinclair, M. F., Christenson, S. L., Evelo, D. L., & Hurley, C. M. (1998). Dropout prevention for youth with disabilities: Efficacy of a sustained school engagement procedure. *Exceptional Children, 65*(1), 7-21.

Skiba, R. J. (2000). Zero tolerance, zero evidence: An analysis of school disciplinary practice. Retrieved from Indiana University Web site at *www.indiana.edu/~safeschl/ztze.pdf.*

Sprague, J., Walker, H., Golly, A., White, K., Myers, D. R., & Shannon, T. (2002). Translating research into effective practice: The effects of a universal staff and student intervention on key indicators of school safety and discipline. *Education and Treatment of Children, 24*(4), 495-511.

Sprague, J. R., & Golly, A. (2005). *Best Behavior: Building positive behavior support in schools.* Longmont, Colorado: Sopris West Educational Services.

Sprague, J. R., & Nishioka, V. (2003/2004). Skills for Success: A three-tiered approach to positive behavior supports. *Impact,* 16-17 & 35.

Sprague, J. R., Sugai, G., & Walker, H. (1998). Antisocial behavior in schools. In F. M. Gresham (Ed.), *Handbook of child behavior therapy* (pp. 451-474). New York: Plenum.

Sprague, J. R., & Walker, H. M. (2005). *Safe and healthy schools: Practical prevention strategies.* New York: Guilford Press.

Sugai, G., & Horner, R. (2002). The evolution of discipline practices: School-wide positive behavior support. *Child and Family Behavior Therapy, 24,* 23-50.

Sugai, G., Horner, R. H., & Gresham, F. (2002). Behaviorally effective environments. In Walker, Shinn, & G. Stoner (Eds.), *Interventions for academic and behavior problems II: Preventive and remedial approaches.* Bethesda, MD: National Association for School Psychologists.

Taylor-Greene, S., Brown, D., Nelson, L., Langton, J., Glassman, T., Cohen, J., et al. (1997). School-wide behavioral support: Starting the year off right. *Journal of Behavioral Education, 7*(1), 99-112.

Tobin, T., & Sprague, J. (2003). Alternative educational programs: Accommodating tertiary level, at-risk students. In M. R. Shinn, G. Stoner, & Walker (Eds.), *Interventions for academic and behavior problems II: Preventive and remedial approaches* (Second ed.). Silver Springs, MD: National Association of School Psychologists (NASP).

Tobin, T. J., & Sugai, G. M. (1999). Using sixth-grade school records to predict school violence, chronic discipline problems, and high school outcomes. *Journal of Emotional and Behavioral Disorders, 4*(2), 82-94.

Tolan, P., & Guerra, N. (1994). *What works in reducing adolescent violence: An empirical review of the field.* Chicago: Center for the Study and Prevention of Violence.

Walker, H. M. (1995). *The acting-out child: Coping with classroom disruption* (Second ed.). Longmont, CO: Sopris West.

Walker, H. M. (1997). *The acting-out child: Coping with classroom disruption* (Second ed.). Boston: Sopris West.

Walker, H. M., Hops, H., & Greenwood, C. R. (1988). *RECESS: Reprogramming environmental contingencies for effective social skills.* Seattle: Educational Achievement Systems.

Walker, H. M., Horner, R. H., Sugai, G., Bullis, M., Sprague, J. R., & Bricker, D., et al. (1996). Integrated approaches to preventing antisocial behavior patterns among school-age children and youth. *Journal of Emotional & Behavioral Disorders, 4*(4), 194-209.

Chapter Four

Data-based Decision-making: What Data Do We Collect and How Do We Use It?

After reading this chapter, you will be able to:

➤ discuss the importance of data collection under an RTI approach for behavior;

➤ discuss the types of data that are collected under an RTI approach for behavior;

➤ discuss the types of decisions that are made under an RTI approach for behavior;

➤ describe how to chart student progress to make data-based decision-making easy; and

➤ provide case examples with data from actual students to demonstrate how to make data-based decisions.

Perhaps more than anything else, RTI represents a data-based decision-making framework. The decisions to be made under RTI are based on data rather than on a staff member's or parent's opinion, a student's reputation, or what the staff member wants to do with the student (e.g., removal from the classroom). The adage "garbage in, garbage out" applies to the data collection procedures used in RTI. Thus, for an RTI approach to function properly, you will need to identify user-friendly and technically sound data collection procedures. One of the first steps, then, to undertake when starting an RTI approach for behavior is to select the data collection procedures that will serve as a basis for making data-based decisions. Data must not only be collected on the student's response to the positive behavior supports, but also on how well the behavior supports are being implemented. Collectively, data in these areas will allow your staff to make educationally valid and legally defensible decisions when selecting, maintaining, modifying, and intensifying behavior supports according to student need. The fundamental notion when making RTI-based decisions is that "in God we trust, for everything else we need data."

Collect the Right Data: Progress Monitoring Data on Student Social Behavior

At the heart of any RTI approach, is a reliable and valid method for measuring student progress. "Progress monitoring is defined as a scientifically based practice that is used to assess students' academic and/or behavior performance and evaluate the effectiveness of instruction or intervention" (National Center on Student Progress Monitoring, 2008). Progress monitoring requires frequent and repeated collection of data. The data that result from progress monitoring will help you and your school staff to make online, formative evaluations of students' response to intervention. Formative evaluation refers to the process of providing ongoing feedback on performance and making ongoing alterations to instruction or intervention. To be useful in formative evaluation, progress monitoring tools must meet technical adequacy standards (reliability and validity), must be sensitive to short-term changes in performance, and must be time-efficient so that teachers can monitor student progress frequently (1-2 times per week). Summative evaluation, on the other hand, involves making judgments about the effectiveness and overall worth of an intervention or a program at its conclusion. You and your staff cannot afford to use a system that relies on summative evaluations of student performance. Doing so, potentially squanders away precious resources and time by continuing to implement ineffective interventions that could have otherwise been altered or discontinued if data were collected and decisions made on an ongoing basis. In short, progress monitoring data makes it possible to make proactive decisions to select, change, or titrate interventions based on how well the student responds to those interventions.

Progress monitoring, when carried out correctly and systematically, will result in desirable outcomes for both your staff and the students they serve. These outcomes include: (a) data-based decision-making; (b) enhanced learning or behavior; (c) greater accountability via documentation of student progress; and (d) more efficient and effective communication between school staff members, parents, and students. Indeed, research has demonstrated the importance of measuring student progress objectively and using those data to determine when and how to adjust academic or behavior support programs. This research indicates that frequent measurement and responsive use of that information in instructional decision-making can enhance teacher planning and student outcomes (e.g., Fuchs, Deno, & Mirkin, 1984; Fuchs, Fuchs, Hamlett, & Stecker, 1991; Jones & Krouse, 1988).

Curriculum-Based Measurement (CBM) probes are now considered to be among the most highly regarded assessment tools for continuous progress monitoring to quantify student performance in reading, mathematics, spelling, and written expression in short-term interventions (Deno, 1985; Good & Kaminski, 2002). Based on over 25 years of systematic research, CBM has been shown to provide reliable and valid measures of general achievement (e.g., reading, mathematics, and written language) that are sensitive to student improvement when used to monitor progress.

Unfortunately, there is no "CBM analogue" for dependably measuring students' response to short-term interventions in the area of social skills and problem behaviors. And, there is no widely agreed-upon method for how to best monitor the progress of students' social behavior, although several measurement procedures have been recommended for this purpose. These shortcomings are likely due to the complex and varied nature of problem behavior and motivation. Nevertheless, the primary methods used in research and practice to monitor the progress of students' social behavior are *Systematic Direct Observation*, *Direct Behavior Ratings*, and *Office Discipline Referrals*. Each of these methods has their own strengths and weaknesses. Your task as an administrator is to weigh the strengths and weaknesses of each of these methods and determine which method best meets your needs and will likely be implemented correctly by your staff.

Systematic Direct Observation

In systematic direct observation, someone other than the classroom teacher (e.g., school psychologist, behavior specialist, school counselor) enters a classroom to observe and record or rate the behavior of a target student. In contrast to naturalistic forms of observation, systematic direct observation requires that (a) the observer select the behavior(s), time, and place for observations prior to collecting data; (b) behaviors are defined in clear and concise language so that two laypersons would agree on the occurrence/non-occurrence of the target behaviors; (c) standardized procedures are used to collect the data; and (d) standardized procedures are used to score and summarize the data (Salvia & Ysseldyke, 2004). One of the significant advantages of systematic direct observation is that the behavior is recorded in a natural setting as it occurs (e.g., classroom, playground, cafeteria), thereby providing the most direct source of behavioral information (Cone, 1978). Systematic direct observation also is capable of being repeatedly conducted — several times a day, if needed — which is a requisite feature of a progress monitoring tool. Despite the advantages of using direct observation methods, you should be aware of the disadvantages of this approach. First, the performance of a school observation is more costly in terms of time, money, and resources than other measurement methods, such as Direct Behavior Ratings or tracking office discipline referrals. Second, systematic direct observation captures a limited sample of behavior that may or may not be representative of the student's performance throughout the day or week. Nevertheless, if you have the person power to conduct systematic direct observations, then it is a viable option as a progress monitoring tool for social behavior.

An example of a systematic direct observation is the Behavioral Observation of Students in Schools (BOSS; Shapiro, 2003). The BOSS is used to record data on the extent to which students are actively or passively engaged in activities and how often they engage in off-task behaviors. While the BOSS is an excellent instrument for recording on- and off-task classroom behaviors, it does not capture the full range of problem behaviors exhibited by students, making it difficult to track progress in certain aspects of maladaptive and adaptive behavior. Therefore, the Student Observation Rating Form (SORF) was developed by Cook and Thornton (2007) to include behavioral response categories that are representative of the majority of problem and prosocial behaviors that are likely to be seen in schools. Unlike most systematic direct observation systems, an advantage of the BOSS is that comes with software that can be uploaded on to a PDA and computer, which streamlines the data collection and scoring process. Only the SORF is discussed in detail. (For additional information on systematic direct observation you should read the article by Robert J. Volpe, James C. DiPerna, John M. Hintze, and Edward S. Shapiro (2005), which includes an excellent review of seven systematic direct observation coding systems.)

The SORF is designed for a 15-minute classroom observation with 15-second intervals. The SORF includes five behavioral response categories: (1) Academic Engagement (AE), (2) Off-task (OFFT), (3) Disruptive Behaviors (DB), (4) Negative Social Interactions (NSI), and (5) Positive Social Interactions (PSI). Figure 1, next page, illustrates the SORF. AE and OFFT are mutually exclusive categories and are recorded at the beginning of every 15-second interval (known as momentary time sampling). This means that the observer records the student as "academically engaged" or "off-task," even though the student may disengage from or become engaged in academics following the beginning of the interval. DB, NSI and ASI are recorded throughout the 15-second interval (known as partial interval recording). That is, if at any point during the interval the student engages in one of the three behaviors, it is marked down as an occurrence. The SORF also is used to collect data on an average peer and the whole class for purposes of comparison. For the peer, observers are instructed to identify an average student behavior-wise — not the best student nor the worse — in the class. This student's behavior is then observed every fourth interval and recorded according to the same guidelines as the target student. During this same interval, observers make a subjective recording regarding classwide behavior. Specifically, classwide behavior is considered to exist within any behavioral response category if three or more of the non-target students are observed exhibiting the behavior during the interval. Thus, if at a glance three students are off-task at the beginning of the interval, then off-task is marked down. The peer and classwide data allow staff to identify whether the problem is specific to the target student or to the class more broadly. Systematic direct observation represents only one method that can be used to measure student progress. Other approaches have been developed and used with the limitations of systematic direct observation in mind.

Figure 1

Student Observation Rating Form

Name of Student:_____   Date:_____   Grade:____

Name of Teacher:_____   Subject:_____

Time:_____

Directions: Identify the target student and record the behaviors. At the very beginning of the interval, record whether the student is academically engaged or off-task. Then throughout the remainder of the interval record whether the student exhibits disruptive behaviors, negative social interactions, and/or appropriate social interactions (see below for definitions of each variable). You also will be recording the behavior of a peer every fourth interval. Pick a peer that is an average student — not the best or worst behaved — to observe. You will be making a rating based on the overall class performance on every fourth interval as well. You will mark an X in the class portion only if three or more students are observed to be engaging in the particular behavior. For academic engagement and off-task, do not mark the class as academically engaged if three or more students are off-task; simply mark off-task at the beginning of the interval. The same recording format is followed for recording class behaviors as is used for recording the target student and an average peer's behavior. The peer and class recording will serve as a comparison to evaluate whether the student's behavior is improving in the desired direction.

Interval	AE	OFFT	DB	NSI	ASI
:15					
:30					
:45					
1:00 Peer / Class					
1:15					
1:30					
1:45					
2:00 Peer / Class					
2:15					
2:30					
2:45					

continues

continued

Interval	AE	OFFT	DB	NSI	ASI
3:00 Peer / Class					
3:15					
3:30					
3:45					
4:00 Peer / Class					
4:15					
4:30					
4:45					
5:00 Peer / Class					
5:15					
5:30					
5:45					
6:00 Peer / Class					
6:15					
6:30					
6:45					
7:00 Peer / Class					
7:15					
7:30					
7:45					

continues

continued

Interval	AE	OFFT	DB	NSI	ASI
8:00 Peer / Class					
8:15					
8:30					
8:45					
9:00 Peer / Class					
9:15					
9:30					
9:45					
10:00 Peer / Class					
10:15					
10:30					
10:45					
11:00 Peer / Class					
11:15					
11:30					
11:45					
12:00 Peer / Class					
12:15					
12:30					
12:45					

continues

continued

Interval	AE	OFFT	DB	NSI	ASI
13:00 Peer / Class	/	/	/	/	/
13:15					
13:30					
13:45					
14:00 Peer / Class	/	/	/	/	/
14:15					
14:30					
14:45					
15:00 Peer / Class	/	/	/	/	/
15:15					
15:30					
15:45					
TOTAL Number Target Student					
Percentage of Intervals Target Student (#/48)					
TOTAL Number Peer					
Percentage of Intervals Peer (#/15)					
TOTAL Number Class					
Percentage of Intervals Class (#/15)					

Behavioral Definitions:

1. **Academic Engagement (AE):** is defined as times when the student is working on the academic task at hand. Examples of academic engagement included: writing, reading aloud, raising a hand and waiting patiently, talking to the teacher or other student about assigned material, and looking things up that are relevant to the assignment. IMPORTANT - **AE** is recorded at the very beginning of each interval; not during the middle of it.

2. **Off-Task (OFFT):** is defined as when a student is not engaged in the academic task at hand, because he or she is staring off, talking to other students about non-academic things, and being disruptive. IMPORTANT - **OFFT** is recorded at the very beginning of each interval; not during the middle of it. Also, a student cannot be academically engaged and off-task at the same time; the two categories are mutually exclusive.

3. **Disruptive Behavior (DB):** is defined as behaviors that are not related to the task at hand and are disruptive to learning or the classroom environment, but do not pose immediate danger to the other peers, teachers, or property (e.g., call outs, talking to peer when not permitted, out of seat, behavior that draws other peers off-task, playing with object).

4. **Negative Social Interaction (NSI):** is defined as negative behaviors that are directed toward others that include biting others, hitting others, pinching, cursing, or verbally or physically threatening or teasing other students.

5. **Appropriate Social Interaction (ASI)** is defined as positive behaviors that are directed toward others that include saying thank you, sharing a pencil, picking an object up and handing it to peer, raising hand and waiting patiently for help, and other positive behaviors that help diffuse a negative situation (e.g., ignoring name calling).

Direct Behavior Rating

In light of the limited feasibility of systematic direct observation as a progress monitoring tool, a group of researchers lead by Sandra Chafouleas from the University of Connecticut developed a hybrid measure that combines aspects of behavior rating scales and systematic direct observation to monitor the progress of student social behavior: Direct Behavior Ratings (DBR). Research has demonstrated that DBRs correlate strongly with systematic direct observation data and school staff view them highly acceptable and easy to complete (Chafouleas, McDougal, Riley-Tillman, Panahon, & Hilt, 2004; Chafouleas et al., 2002). Chafouleas and colleagues have defined DBRs as "performance-based recording procedures used to collect teacher ratings of a student specific to a predetermined set of behaviors" (p. 540). A good DBR has the following four characteristics: (1) the behavior of interest is defined in clear and measurable language; (2) the recordings of student behavior are completed according to standardized instructions; (3) the DBR should be used during a specific time and place; and (4) the data resulting from the DBR are summarized and reviewed on an ongoing basis.

An obvious question is: how do you design a DBR form for data collection purposes? Chafouleas, Riley-Tillman, and Sugai (2007) have outlined a three-step process that is amenable to just about any behavior your staff members would be interested in monitoring. The first step is to identify the target behavior(s). DBRs are flexible in that they can be designed to assess increases in positive behaviors (e.g., On-Task: the student was working on the assigned activity) or decreases in negative behaviors (e.g., Verbal Aggression: the student yelled at, cursed at, threatened, or teased a peer). Generally, you will want to have your staff select no more than three target behaviors to include in the DBR. Table 1, next page, includes a list of common behaviors to include in a DBR. Once the target behaviors have been identified, the next step is to develop the scale on which the behavior will be rated.

Table 1

Possible DBR Target Behaviors

Behavior of Interest	Description of Behavior
Positive/Appropriate Behaviors	
On-Task	The student was working on the assigned activity.
Raises Hand	The student raised hand and was called on before responding.
Hands to Self	The student kept his/her hands to self.
Used Appropriate Voice	The student used appropriate voice tone in class during conversations.
Compliance	The student responded to teacher requests or directives within 5 seconds.
Negative/Inappropriate Behaviors	
Disruptive Behavior	The student disrupted the class by getting out of seat, talking out loud, making noises with object, or throwing things at classmates.
Verbal Aggression	The student yelled at, cursed at, threatened, or teased a peer.
Physical Aggression	The student hit, pushed, pinched, slapped, or scratched a peer.
Non-compliance	The student failed to respond to the teacher's request or directive within 10 seconds.
Crying	The student cried or had tears in eyes.

There are several options to select from when considering the scale for rating. The most popular scaling technique is a Likert-type scale. A Likert-type scale has your teacher or support staff rate the item according to the level s/he thinks is most true or accurate. Generally, there are at-least five levels to the rating. Chafouleas and colleagues recommend 10 levels or increments. For example, if the target behavior of interest was Compliance, an example Likert-type scale would be as follows:

Compliance: The student responded to teacher requests or directives within 5-seconds

1	2	3	4	5	6	7	8	9	10
(Never)					(Sometimes)				(Always)

Another scaling technique is to use a continuous line. A continuous line includes numbers or percentages from zero to 100 and the teacher or support staff marks the point in the continuum s/he thinks most accurately captures the student's behavior for the specified time period. Consider the target behavior *On-Task* behavior as an example. At the end of the day, the teacher would mark on the continuous line the percentage of time s/he believes the student was on-task for that day.

On-Task: The student was working on the assigned activity

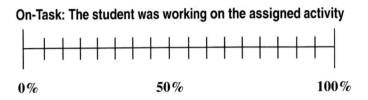

Yet another approach to scaling, especially for younger students or students who have a difficult time understanding the meaning of ratings, is the use of smiley faces. This is particularly useful if the data are going to be shared with the younger students or students with limited comprehension skills.

Hands to self: I kept my hands to self

Using a yes/no (occurrence/nonoccurrence) checklist format also is a scaling option, especially for behaviors that do not occur regularly. The developmental functioning of the student should be taken into account when developing the scale.

It also is important to consider who will be responsible for completing the DBR. Typically, the classroom teacher is the person who is responsible for completing the DBR. However, students with behavior problems have a way of putting tremendous stress on their classroom teachers and, consequently, the students' reputations have a way of being factored into the rating process, which may mask intervention effects. If there is reason to believe that the classroom teacher will not complete the DBR accurately, then you may want to consider someone else who interacts with the student on a regular basis.

The data gathered from the DBRs can be easily quantified and summarized to make decisions. The methods that can be used to summarize systematic direct observation data also can be applied to DBR data. (Later in the chapter a technique for summarizing and displaying the data for purposes of making decisions is discussed.) Figure 2, next page, provides an illustration of a sample DBR.

Figure 2

Direct Behavior Rating Form

Student:_____

Date of rating:_____   Time of rating:_____

First Target Behavior: <u>Raising Hand: "the student raises his hand before speaking aloud in class."</u>

| 0   1   2   3   4   5   6   7   8   9 |

(0 times)   (9 times)

Second Target Behavior: <u>Verbal aggression: "the student yells, calls names, curses, or makes other noises that would be considered aggressive behavior."</u>

| 0   1   2   3   4   5   6   7   8   9 |

(0 times)   (9 times)

Overall daily behavior rating: <u>Based on your judgment of the student's behavior today, how true is this statement: "the student did better today than before the intervention was implemented."</u>

| 0   1   2   3   4   5   6   7 |

(very not true)   (very true)

Comments:

Office Discipline Referrals

Although not a direct measure of behavior, office discipline referrals have been used to assess student social behavior. Office discipline referrals Research has shown ODR data to be useful decision-making purposes (Horner & Sugai, 2001; Irvin, Tobin, Sprague, Sugai, & Vincent, 2004; Sprague, Sugai, Horner, & Walker, 1999). The School-Wide Information System (SWIS™, *www.swis.org*) is a Web-based information system designed to help school personnel to manage and use office referral data to design schoolwide and individual student interventions. While SWIS™ is designed to generally monitor behavior functioning at the school level (e.g., the number of office discipline referrals per month, the type of problem behaviors leading to office referrals, the locations of problem behavior events, problem behavior events by time of day, and the students contributing to office discipline referrals), it also can be used to monitor data at the individual level (the number of discipline referrals for a student each week, the type of problem behaviors leading to office referrals for each student, and the time of day the student is most likely to receive an office discipline referral). The major limitation with ODR data is that they generally are good at measuring *externalizing* problems (e.g., verbal aggression, disruptive behavior, off-task, etc.), but poor at capturing *internalizing* behavior patterns (e.g., withdrawn, anxious, depressed, etc.). ODR data also are limited as a progress monitoring tool in the sense that minor behavior problems often go undetected, given that ODRs are typically reserved for more intense behavior problems that warrant assistance from someone outside of the classroom. Also, whether a student receives an ODR is often dependent on a teacher's tolerance level, which can fluctuate day-to-day and differ from teacher-to-teacher. Finally, ODRs will be more reliable (accurate) if class- versus office-managed behaviors are clearly defined, and teachers receive regular feedback on their patterns of office referrals compared to others in the building. Even if you do not adopt *www.swis.org*, it is possible to view a list of standard reports generated by the database at the site. There is a demonstration data set available on the site and the username and login are supplied. We recommend that these types of reports are shared at least monthly to your entire staff, and the individual student reports can be valuable in problem analysis or progress monitoring for individual students. Figure 3, next page, illustrates a comprehensive behavior incident report, and additional examples can be found at *www.swis.org/resources*.

Figure 3

Office Referral Form

Name: _____	**Location**	
Date: _____ Time: _____	Playground	Library
Teacher: _____	Cafeteria	Bathroom
Grade: K 1 2 3 4 5 6 7 8	Hallway	Arrival/Dismissal
Referring Staff: _____	Classroom	Other _____

Minor Problem Behavior	**Major Problem Behavior**	**Possible Motivation**
Inappropriate language	Abusive language	Obtain peer attention
Physical contact	Fighting/ Physical aggression	Obtain adult attention
Defiance	Overt Defiance	Obtain items/activities
Disruption	Harassment/Bullying	Avoid Peer(s)
Dress Code	Dress Code	Avoid Adult
Property misuse	Tardy	Avoid task or activity
Tardy	Inappropriate Display Aff.	Don't know
Electronic Violation	Electronic Violation	Other _____
Other _____	Lying/ Cheating	
	Skipping class	
	Other _____	

Administrative Decision

Loss of privilege	Individualized instruction
Time in office	In-school suspension (____hours/ days)
Conference with student	Out of school suspension (_____ days)
Parent Contact	Other _____

Others involved in incident: None Peers Staff Teacher Substitute
Unknown Other

Other comments: _____

I need to talk to the students' teacher   I need to talk to the administrator

Parent Signature: _____   **Date:** _____

All minors are filed with classroom teacher. Three minors equal a major.
All majors require administrator consequence, parent contact, and signature.

Intervention Fidelity

Intervention fidelity refers to the extent to which the behavior supports and services are implemented as intended or designed (Fixen et al., 2005; Gresham, 1989). Fidelity of implementation has been referred to in the scientific research as treatment integrity, procedural reliability, or treatment fidelity. Intervention fidelity data represent a vital ingredient in any RTI-based decision-making system. Failure to document whether positive behavior supports were implemented with fidelity poses serious limitations to your staff's ability to draw valid conclusions about a student's response to intervention. That is, without data on the fidelity of implementation of the behavioral supports, school teams will be unable to determine whether a student failed to respond well to the intervention because it was implemented inaccurately or inconsistently, or whether the actual student resisted an otherwise ineffective, well-implemented intervention. The risks inherent in not collecting fidelity of implementation data are two-fold. The collection of treatment integrity data serves an additional function as a school administrator: It allows you to hold your staff accountable for implementing evidence-based practices.

Intervention fidelity, sometimes referred to as treatment fidelity in the clinical psychology literature (Moncher & Prinz, 1991) or procedural reliability in the applied behavior analysis literature (Peterson, Homer, & Wonderlich, 1982), refers to the extent to which an intervention plan is implemented as designed. Research has demonstrated that poor treatment integrity is an aspect of service delivery that often undermines the efficacy of interventions and supports delivered in natural educational settings (Wickstrom, Jones, LaFleur, & Witt, 1998). As a result, when a particular tier of supports results in poor outcomes, the first question that the school team must address before any other conclusion can be reached is, "Was the intervention implemented with integrity?" Noell and Witt's (1999) research on the effects of intervention delivered via a consultative process underscores the importance of treatment integrity data. These authors revealed that academic and behavioral interventions were much more effective in producing desirable student outcomes when implemented with higher levels of integrity. Without the collection of treatment integrity data, it is impossible for the school team to determine whether the lack of response on the part of the student was due to poor implementation of an otherwise effective intervention, or whether there was resistance on the part of the student to a high-quality intervention implemented with fidelity.

There are two dimensions that are important when examining the extent to which an intervention is implemented as planned. These two dimensions are consistency and accuracy. Consistency refers to whether the intervention is routinely implemented day-to-day. Accuracy refers to whether intervention is implemented correctly on a daily basis. Treatment integrity may indicate a problem with consistency, accuracy, or both. For example, if a teacher did well at implementing the intervention on Monday through Wednesday, but did poorly later in the week, then there would be a problem with consistency. On the other hand, if the teacher regularly failed to implement particular components of the intervention every day of the week, then there would a problem with accuracy. The worst-case scenario is when the implementer has problems with both consistency and accuracy of implementation. There are several different methods for collecting data on treatment integrity: (a) direct observation, (b) checklists, (c) self-report, and (d) permanent product.

Direct observation of intervention fidelity is perhaps the best approach to assessing whether the intervention is being implemented as planned. This method requires someone other than the implementer of the positive behavior supports to go into the setting and time in which the intervention is being delivered, and objectively observe and document whether the intervention is being implemented consistently and accurately. Assessment of intervention fidelity is typically accomplished by directly observing teachers during plan implementation and calculating the percentage of treatment steps implemented correctly.

Permanent Product

Permanent product data are by-products of behavior that can be used to assess the effectiveness of intervention (e.g., number of chairs turned over during an aggressive episode) or, in this case, intervention fidelity. An advantage of permanent product data is that the products that result from delivering the positive behavior supports are permanent. Permanent product data also can serve the secondary function of holding staff and students accountable for implementing or participating in the intervention. A prime example of using permanent product data to assess intervention fidelity is the implementation of a self-monitoring protocol. These also are known as point charts, school-home notes, and check-in/check-out point cards (Hawken & Horner, 2003). Self-monitoring requires the student to repeatedly monitor his/her behavior at scheduled or random time points and mark down on a chart how well s/he is meeting behavioral expectations. Teachers conduct periodic honesty checks of the student's responses by marking on the chart whether the student is providing truthful responses. The chart is then turned in at the end of the day to review student performance for the day, provide feedback, and deliver predetermined reward if goal was met. The self-monitoring chart is a permanent product of the intervention and, therefore, can be used to assess whether the self-monitoring intervention was implemented with fidelity. For instance, from the chart one can determine whether the (a) student marked down responses at each of the scheduled self-monitoring time points; (b) teacher conducted honesty checks of the student's responses; (c) self-monitoring chart was turned in; (d) feedback was provided; and (e) reward delivered, if goal was met.

Self-Report

Another approach to collecting intervention fidelity data is to have the intervention implementers to rate or check off how well they are implementing components of the intervention. This approach is preferred less than the other approaches because research has shown that implementers tend to over-rate how well they implemented the intervention. The research by Wickstrom, Jones, LaFleur, and Witt (1998) demonstrates the weakness of using self-report for collecting intervention fidelity data. Whereas teachers reported that they were implementing interventions with over 70 percent integrity, direct observation data revealed that teachers actually were implementing the interventions with less than 10 percent fidelity. Despite the limitations of self-report, it is often a more feasible approach to collecting intervention fidelity data than other approaches. And, some intervention fidelity data is better than having no data.

There are few different ways you could go about collecting self-report intervention fidelity data. One way to go about it is to have the intervention implementer rate the fidelity of implementation on a 5-point scale (see Figure 4, next page). Another way to collect self-report intervention fidelity data is to have the intervention implementer complete a simple yes/no checklist for each of the intervention components.

Figure 4

Example Intervention Fidelity Self-Report Ratings

How well did you implement the mentoring aspect of the Check in/Check out intervention?

1	2	3	4	5
(not at all)	(poorly)	(okay)	(well)	(perfectly)

Did you provide four behavior specific praise statements to the student for every disapproving statement?

1	2	3	4	5
(none)	(not so much)	(not quite)	(almost)	(yes, at-least 4:1)

How well did you and the student carry out the self-monitoring intervention?

1	2	3	4	5
(not at all as planned)		(somewhat as planned)		(exactly as planned)

What percent of the behavior support plan components were implemented as planned?

1	2	3	4	5
(0-20%)	(21-40%)	(41-60%)	(61-80%)	(81-100%)

Performance Feedback

What do you do when the treatment integrity data indicate that the supports are being poorly implemented? The quick answer to this question is *performance feedback*. Performance feedback is the process of providing specific information to the implementer about his/her performance implementing the intervention. Everyone enjoys a little bit of positive recognition. So, it is important to not only point out the implementer's flaws with implementing the supports, but also his/her strengths. This will increase your effectiveness. Also, make sure the staff person has the necessary resources to implement the intervention effectively. Numerous studies have documented the benefits of performance feedback to increase treatment integrity (Codding, Feinburg, Dunn, & Pace, 2005; Hagermoser-Sanetti, Luselli, & Handler, 2007; Mortenson & Witt, 1998; Noell, Duhon, Gatti, & Connell, 2002; Noell, Witt, Gilbertson, Ranier, & Freeland, 1997; Witt, Noell, LaFleur, & Mortenson, 1997). These studies indicate that once the interventions were implemented with greater integrity, improved student outcomes were observed.

Summarizing Intervention Fidelity Data

The whole point behind collecting intervention fidelity data is to make legally defensible and educationally valid decisions. Therefore, beyond merely collecting the intervention fidelity data, the school team will want to summarize and review the data on an ongoing basis along with the student response data. There are several ways in which the intervention fidelity data can be summarized. Perhaps the most useful method for summarizing the data is to plug it in to a Day of the Week by Intervention Component Intervention Fidelity Table (see Figure 5, next page); this is, of course, if you choose to have intervention fidelity data collected on a daily basis. This table will allow your staff to calculate and review daily levels of fidelity across intervention components and the fidelity of each of the intervention components across days of the week. These data can be compared with the student's progress monitoring data to determine whether there are higher rates of problem behavior on days when the intervention was implemented poorly or when certain intervention components were not implemented accurately. The data also can be aggregated to produce a total intervention fidelity index to assess the overall fidelity of implementation. In sum, using this table to summarize the intervention fidelity data enables the school team to glean important information that can be used to identify where and when there are particular breakdowns in the delivery of the positive behavior supports.

Figure 5

Daily and Component Intervention Fidelity Form

Student: _____

Implementer: _____

Describe intervention:

List the components of the intervention:

1.
2.
3.
4.

Week of: _____

Intervention Components	Monday	Tuesday	Wednesday	Thursday	Friday	Component Integrity
(1)	Yes No	Yes No	Yes No	Yes No	Yes No	
(2)	Yes No	Yes No	Yes No	Yes No	Yes No	
(3)	Yes No	Yes No	Yes No	Yes No	Yes No	
(4)	Yes No	Yes No	Yes No	Yes No	Yes No	
Daily Integrity						

Note: For each day, simply mark yes or no as to whether the particular intervention component was implemented with integrity. At the end of the week, calculate the column and row totals to assess daily and component integrity.

Consider the intervention fidelity data included in Figure 6, next page, as an example. The data indicate that the intervention was implemented reasonably well on Monday through Wednesday, but not well on Thursday and Friday. Based on these data, the school team should explore what about Thursday and Friday is related to poorer implementation of the intervention. It could be that there are different activities scheduled on Thursday and Friday, such as going to the library or computer time, that disrupts the implementation of the intervention. Also, the data in Figure 6, next page, indicate that the intervention component daily delivery of reward or loss of points was implemented poorly. Here, the school team could use this data to consult with the teacher to provide performance feedback and help support the teacher with implementing this critical component of the intervention. In any case, when the intervention fidelity data indicate that the positive behavior supports are not being implemented consistently or accurately, then "do not pass go, and do not collect $200." Meaning, before any other decisions are made, data must indicate that the intervention is being implemented with fidelity. The student cannot respond to an intervention that is not implemented!

Daily and Component Intervention Fidelity Form

Figure 6

<u>Student</u>: Jim Matthews

<u>Implementer</u>: Mrs. Grover

<u>Week of</u>: Oct. 24th

Describe intervention: Self-monitoring, behavior specific praise, and daily reward or performance feedback

List the components of the intervention:

1. Morning check in
2. Behavior specific praise
3. Self-monitoring completed
4. Reward delivered or performance feedback

Intervention Components	Monday		Tuesday		Wednesday		Thursday		Friday		Component Integrity
(1) Morning check in	**Yes**	No	**Yes**	No	**Yes**	No	Yes	**No**	Yes	**No**	60%
(2) Behavior specific praise	**Yes**	No	**Yes**	No	**Yes**	No	**Yes**	No	**Yes**	No	100%
(3) Self-monitoring form completed	**Yes**	No	Yes	**No**	**Yes**	No	Yes	**No**	Yes	**No**	40%
(4) Reward delivered or performance feedback	**Yes**	No	**Yes**	No	**Yes**	No	Yes	**No**	Yes	**No**	60%
Daily Integrity	100%		75%		100%		25%		25%		**65%**

Note: For each day, simply mark yes or no as to whether the particular intervention component was implemented with integrity. At the end of the week, calculate the column and row totals to assess daily and component integrity.

Data-based Decisions under an RTI Approach for Behavior

Time is an important consideration when making decisions in an RTI approach for behavior. The length of time a student is exposed to Tier II or III positive behavior supports is an important consideration. Different students will likely respond differently to the same positive behavior supports. For example, while one student may respond immediately to the Tier II supports, another student receiving the same supports may demonstrate a delayed response to the supports. Given the variability in student response, you should adopt a length of time criterion to ensure that students are provided a sufficient amount of time to demonstrate adequate response to the positive behavior supports. The research does not provide much guidance on the optimal length of time positive behavior supports should be implemented. In the absence of research-based guidelines, we developed a pragmatic length of time criterion. We recommend that the positive behavior supports are implemented for a minimum of four weeks. Four weeks is an ideal minimal length of time criterion for a number of reasons. First, it allows sufficient time for the student to demonstrate adequate or inadequate response to the supports. Second, four weeks allows school staff to collect at-least four progress monitoring data points to assess level and trend in student response to intervention. Third, within a four-week time period school teams can assess the fidelity of implementation of the positive behavior supports and make adjustments to the intervention or consult with implementers to increase the accuracy and consistency of implementation. The data-based decisions discussed in the following paragraphs are reserved for students who have been identified by the universal screening procedures (Chapter 2) and, therefore, are involved in Tier II or III positive behavior supports.

All decisions are potentially on the table when the school team convenes to review the student's response to intervention. There are four basic data-based decisions that can be made when conducting a formative evaluation of the student's progress: (a) keep current supports in place, (b) modify current supports within the tier, (c) lessen supports by dropping the student down a tier, and (d) intensify supports by bumping the student up a tier. These decisions all assume that the supports have been implemented with fidelity. Therefore, the first thing your school teams will want to consider is whether the supports have been faithfully implemented. Again, the decision-making process *should not* proceed if the behavior supports were not implemented as planned. Once the team is confident that the positive behavior supports were implemented with fidelity (i.e., data indicate that the treatment components were implemented as planned), then the team can examine the student response data and determine the appropriateness of the current supports. Figure 7, next page, represents a data-based decision-making tree that your school teams could use to guide their decision-making.

Figure 7

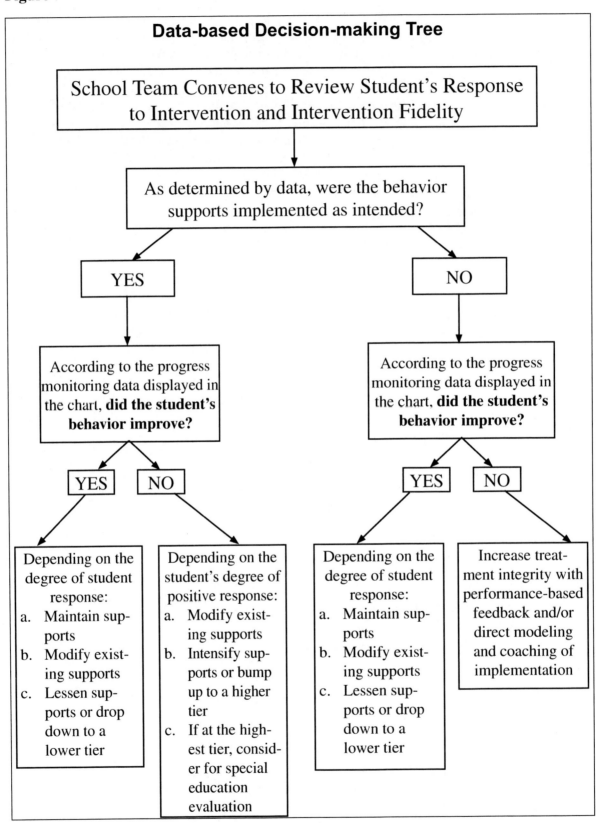

Keeping the current supports in place is a data-based decision that generally is made when the progress monitoring data suggest that the student is responding to the interventions but not necessarily to the degree that would warrant lessening the intensity of supports. For example, a team may decide to keep the current supports in place for a student whose data suggest a decreasing trend in the frequency of his problem behavior from 10 episodes per day during baseline to six episodes per day with Tier II supports. In this case, the team is likely to be somewhat satisfied with the 40 percent decrease in problem behaviors, but would like to continue the implementation of the Tier II supports to see if the student's behavior will reduce in number closer to the school average of two-three problem behaviors per day. Teams also may want to consider keeping the current supports in place for a student who has responded very well, but will likely be unsuccessful with less-intensive supports in place. However, if the student responds well to the current supports for a prolonged period of time, the team will want to consider lessening the intensity of supports by the lowering the student down a tier to avoid having the student become dependent on the supports. However, the beauty of RTI is that it is flexible and can accommodate moving a student down a tier and then back up if the student's behaviors deteriorate and become problematic again.

The decision to *modify current supports* is made when the progress monitoring data indicate that the student has not responded well to the positive behavior supports and the school team believes that a modification or addition to the current behavior supports would improve the student's response to intervention. This is a decision that is made using a combination of student response data (i.e., inadequate response to intervention) and professional judgment (i.e., belief that a change or addition to the intervention will result in improved student response). If the school team has reason to believe that the student may respond better to the current tier of behavior supports with a few modifications or additions, then, for the sake of conserving resources and time, the team should modify the current supports before considering any other option that is on the table.

Lessen the positive behavior supports by dropping the student down a tier is a decision that is made when the progress monitoring data indicate strong response to intervention on the part of the student and the school team is reasonably confident that the student will be able to sustain his/her social behavior performance in a less-intensive tier of supports. This does not have to be an all or none decision. The school team can "test" whether the student is likely to sustain improved behavior by gradually fading the supports. Fading is the systematic process of reducing features of an intervention (e.g., reduction in intervention components or number of days the intervention is implemented) as the student demonstrates skill mastery or acceptable behavior performance. Progress monitoring data will tell you whether the student is sustaining improved behavior as the intervention is faded.

Intensify the positive behavior supports by bumping the student up a tier is a decision reserved when the following conditions are met: (1) student demonstrates persistent non-response to the interventions; (2) intervention fidelity data indicate that the interventions were implemented with fidelity; and (3) the school team is reasonably confident that modifications to the current positive behavior supports will not result in better student response. School team members should not be in a rush to bump up a student a tier. The interventions should be implemented for a minimum of four weeks, but could conceivably last much longer in duration if the team decides so. The team may decide that the student will likely respond well if a different intervention is tried or a modification is made to the current intervention. However, once the team believes they have exhausted all the interventions and supports within a particular tier and the student continues to demonstrate inadequate response, then a decision should be made to bump the student up to a more intensive tier of supports.

Monitoring Student Progress: A Chart Says a Thousand Words

The regular charting or graphing of student response data is a critical component of progress monitoring and data-based decision-making. By charting the data, the school team is able to depict and visually inspect all the progress monitoring data in a single summary chart. From this chart, the team can analyze levels and trends in behavior performance within and across tiers of support to make decisions about whether to maintain, modify, intensify, or lessen behavioral supports. Fuchs and Fuchs' (1986) synthesis of research studies examining the impact of progress monitoring on student outcomes highlights the benefits of charting progress monitoring data. Fuchs and Fuchs aggregated 96 effect sizes (i.e., statistics represent the magnitude of the effect of progress monitoring on student outcomes) from 21 controlled studies to derive an average-weighted effect size of 0.70 for the effect of progress monitoring. This effect size indicates that progress monitoring would likely result in a student gaining 24 percentile rank points on a standardized behavioral outcome measure (e.g., behavior rating scale). However, the most important finding from their research was that which indicated an average effect size of 1.12 when behavior supports were combined with charting progress monitoring data, which represents an extremely powerful and large effect. Thus, charting student progress not only facilitates data-based decision-making, but it is an intervention component capable of improving student outcomes.

A chart paints a clear picture of the student's response to positive behavior supports. In the chart, the student's social behavior performance in Tier I (i.e., baseline) and subsequent tiers of support can be captured in a single representation, allowing school teams to make comparisons within and across particular tiers of support. In this way, a chart does say a thousand words. The charting of progress monitoring data makes the school team's job easy. The team simply adds or has the student add a progress monitoring data point each day or week to the chart, depending on how frequently the data are collected. After three data points are displayed in the chart, there are enough data to assess levels and trends in social behavior performance. The school team can then begin to visually inspect the chart to make decisions about the student's response to intervention.

Figure 8

Sample Progress Monitoring Graph

STUDENT NAME:

INTERVENTION START DATE:

GOAL REVIEW DATE:

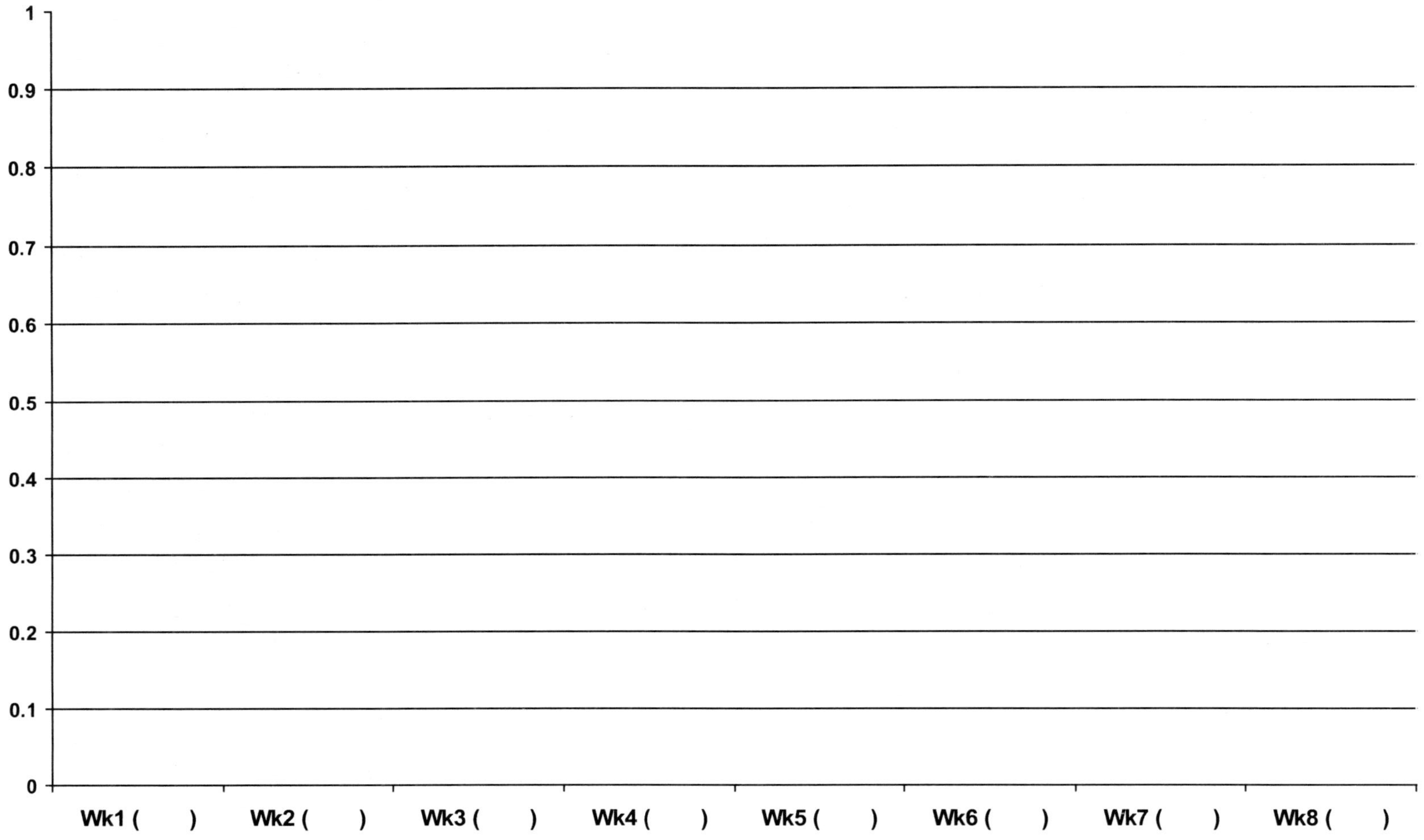

Case Examples

The following are case examples of actual students attending schools in which RTI practices for behavior were being implemented. The decisions represent actual decisions made by school teams to maintain, modify, intensify, or lessen positive behavior supports.

John

John was a 9-year-old African American male who was attending the third grade at an elementary school in a large, urban school district. John's intellectual functioning was judged to be within the average range. He performed above the 40th percentile in both reading and mathematics. John's primary problem in school was that he engaged in high rates of disruptive and off-task behavior compared to other students, which was interfering with his learning and that of others. His disruptive behavior consisted of getting out of seat, making distracting noises with objects, talking with peers about non-academic content, and providing answers without raising his hand.

The universal screening procedures (Chapter 2) implemented in the school identified John as a candidate for Tier II positive behavior supports. The team agreed that John would benefit from more intensive supports beyond what was being provided in Tier I. The school team decided that John would likely benefit from a strict schedule of behavior specific praise to increase the ratio of approving to disapproving statements along with a self-monitoring intervention. Before the Tier II supports were implemented, the school team collected progress monitoring data using the SORF. Given the nature of John's problem behavior, only academic engagement, off-task behavior, and disruptive behavior were used to monitor his progress. The school team developed two goals for John: (1) By October 30, 2005, during class instruction or independent seatwork time, John will be Academically Engaged for 85 percent of the intervals as measured by the SORF; and (2) By October 30, 2005, during class instruction or independent seatwork time, John will engage in Disruptive Behaviors for less than 10 percent of the intervals as measured by the SORF. (John's progress monitoring data are included in Figure 9, next page.)

As you can see, John responded well to the Tier II interventions: increase in academic engagement, decrease in off-task behavior, and decrease in disruptive behavior. The school team convened on October 19th to review intervention fidelity data and John's response to the Tier II positive behavior supports. The intervention fidelity data indicated that the supports were being implemented as planned: behavior specific praise 90 percent fidelity and self-monitoring intervention 88 percent fidelity. Based on John's response to intervention, the school team made the decision to lessen the intensity of the positive behavior supports by returning John to the Tier I level of supports. This decision was reached prior to the date that was set to evaluate John's goal attainment. This decision was based on the fact that John had met both goals and the chart displaying his progress monitoring data demonstrated clear response to intervention. It is important to note that in John's case the collection of intervention fidelity data contributes less for decision-making purposes, since he showed significant response to intervention. That is, the school team was not necessarily concerned, nor should they be, with what was responsible for the desirable changes in John's behavior. Rather, they were simply happy to see that his behavior moved within the range of normal functioning. However, imagine if John would not have responded well to the Tier II supports. In this scenario, the school team would have had a difficult time determining whether John's non-responsiveness was due to poor fidelity of implementation or inadequate response to an ineffective intervention implemented with fidelity. Thus, the importance of collecting intervention fidelity data is not for use when the student responds well to the intervention, but rather preparing for the possibility that the student does not respond well to the intervention. In the next case example of Mary, you will see how important intervention fidelity data is to the decision-making process.

Figure 9

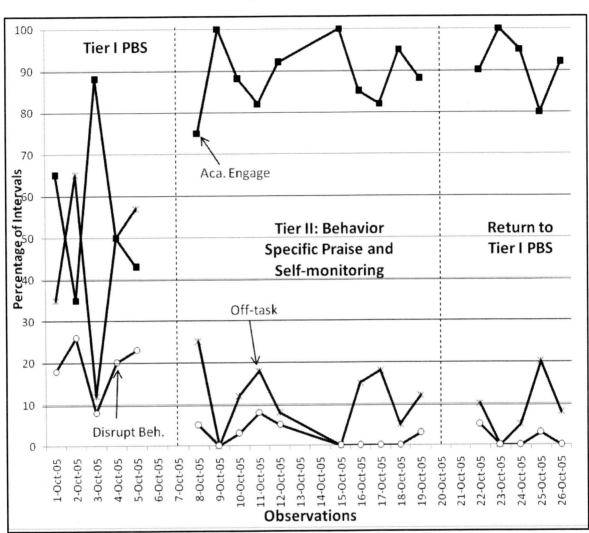

John's Progress Monitoring Data

Mary

Mary was an 11-year-old Caucasian who was attending the fifth grade at an elementary school in a large, urban school district. Prior testing indicated that Mary's intellectual functioning was within the average to low-average range (95 percent Confidence Interval 84–99). Her performance on oral reading fluency passages from Aimsweb indicated that she correctly read at a rate of 52 words per minute on grade-level passages, which placed her in the "at-risk" category for later reading problems. Records review indicated that she had behavior problems since kindergarten. Mary's target behavior was *negative social interactions with peers and adults*, which entailed yelling, name calling, pushing, throwing objects, tattling, and noncompliance to adult directives.

Universal screening procedures, consisting of teacher nominations and the Student Risk Screening Scale (Chapter 2), identified Mary as an inadequate responder to the Tier I positive behavior supports and at risk for developing an emotional and behavioral disorder. The school team determined that Mary was in need of more intensive positive behavior supports. From the menu of Tier II positive behavior supports, the team selected a mentor-based intervention (Check In/Check Out) combined with self-monitoring, since Mary frequently verbalized that she did not feel liked by her peers or the school staff at school. The team collected baseline data every day for a week using a Direct Behavior Rating Form prior to implementing the Tier II interventions, after which they developed two behavioral goals for Mary: (1) By March 27, 2007, throughout all settings in the school, Mary will earn a rating of 3 or less for Negative Social Interactions with Peers as measured by the Direct Behavior Rating Form; and (2) By March 27, 2007, during class instruction or independent seatwork time, Mary will earn a rating of 3 or less for Compliance to Adult Directives as measured by the Direct Behavior Rating Form. In this case, lower scores were indicative of better social interactions with peers and compliance to adult directives. The school team convened after four weeks of implementation of the Tier II supports to review Mary's progress monitoring data, assess her response to the interventions, and make a data-based decision. Mary's progress monitoring data are depicted in Figure 10, next page.

Figure 10

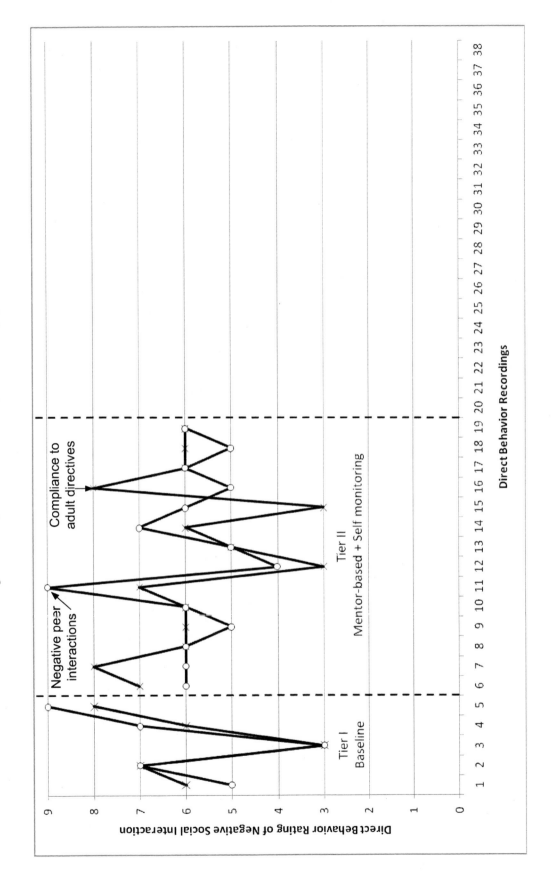

Mary's Response to the Tier II Supports

As you can see, Mary did not respond well to the Tier II interventions. The team reviewed the intervention fidelity data and determined that the mentor-based program and self-monitoring intervention had indeed been implemented accurately and consistently. The team was confident that the data did not support keeping the current interventions in place, and they did not believe modifying the current interventions would facilitate improved student response. The decision, therefore, was made to bump up Mary to Tier III positive behavior supports.

A functional behavior assessment was conducted to identify the function of Mary's negative social interactions. The functional behavior assessment data indicated that the function of Mary's negative social interactions was to escape or avoid unpleasant situations with peers or teachers. Based on this information, a behavior support plan was developed to orchestrate the implementation of specific positive behavior supports and strategies. The supports and strategies included environmental alterations to decrease the likelihood of the problem behavior, the implementation of a strict reinforcement schedule to increase the likelihood of prosocial behavior, the use of positive strategies to respond to the problem behavior, and replacement skills training to teach Mary functionally equivalent replacement behaviors that will enable her to escape/avoid unpleasant situations with peers and adults in a socially acceptable way.

The behavior support plan was implemented for six weeks. Figure 11, next page, depicts Mary's response to the Tier III supports. During the six weeks of implementation, the school team made modifications to the behavior support plan by changing additional aspects of the educational environment and trying different reinforcement procedures, due to the lack of response demonstrated by Mary. The team monitored closely the fidelity of implementation of the behavior support plan throughout the six weeks, and determined that the behavior support plan was implemented accurately and consistently. At this point, the school team concluded that they had made a good attempt at providing Mary with a graduated sequence of high-quality positive behavior supports, yet she continued to engage in negative social interactions and demonstrate a need for additional services and supports. The school team made the decision to refer Mary for special education evaluation under the category of emotional disturbance. Mary was ultimately identified as emotionally disturbed and provided special education and related services.

Figure 11

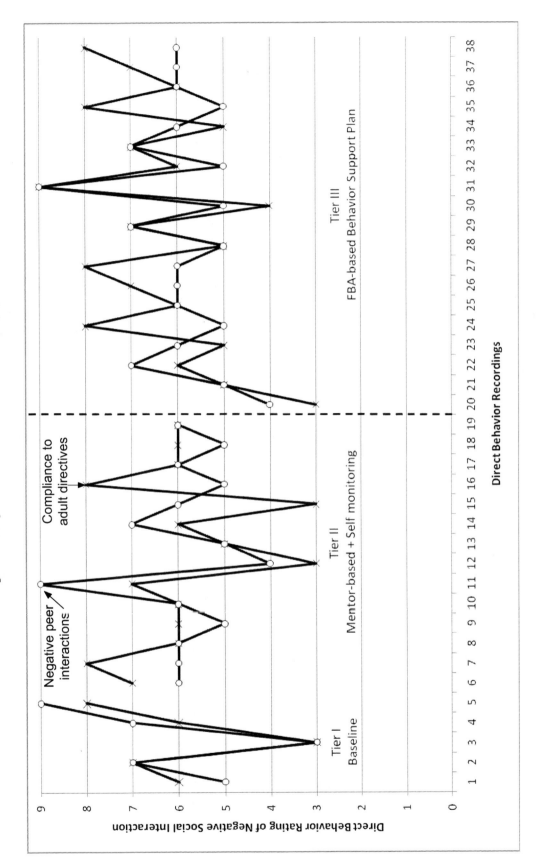

Mary's Response to the Tier III Supports

References

Chafouleas, S., Riley-Tilman, C., & Sugai, G. (2007). *School-based behavior assessment: Informing intervention and instruction.* New York: Guilford Press.

Codding, R. S., Feinburg, A. B., Dunn, E. K., & Pace, G. M. (2005). Effects of immediate performance feedback on implementation of behavior support plans. *Journal of Applied Behavior Analysis, 38,* 205-219.

Cone, J. D. (1978). The behavioral assessment grid (BAG): A conceptual framework and taxonomy. *Behavior Therapy, 9,* 882–888.

Deno, S. L. (1985). Curriculum-based measurement: The emerging alternative. *Exceptional Children, 52,* 219-232.

Fixsen, D. L., Naoom, S. F., Blase, K. A., Friedman, R. M., & Wallace, F. (2005). *Implementation research: A synthesis of the literature.* Tampa, FL: University of South Florida, Louis de la Parte Florida Mental Health Institute, The National Implementation Research Network (FMHI Publication #231). Available at *http://nirn.fmhi.usf.edu.*

Fuchs, L. S., Deno, S. L., & Mirkin, P. K. (1984). Effects of frequent curriculum-based measurement and evaluation of pedagogy, student achievement, and student awareness of learning. *American Educational Research Journal, 21,* 449-460.

Fuchs, L. S., & Fuchs, D. (1986). Effects of systematic formative evaluation: A meta-analysis. *Exceptional Children, 53*(3), 199-208.

Fuchs, L. S., Fuchs, D., Hamlett, C. L., & Stecker, P. M. (1991). Effects of curriculum-based measurement and consultation on teacher planning and student achievement in mathematics operations. *American Educational Research 28,* 617-641.

Good, R. H., & Kaminski, R. A. (Eds.). (2002). *Dynamic indicators of basic early literacy skills* (6th ed.). Eugene, OR: Institute for the Development of Education Achievement.

Gresham, F. M. (1989). Assessment of treatment integrity in school consultation and prereferral intervention. *School Psychology Review, 18,* 37-50.

Hagermoser-Sanetti, L. M., Luiselli, J. K., & Handler, M. W. (2007). Effects of verbal and graphic performance feedback on behavior support plan implementation in a public elementary school. *Behavior Modification, 31,* 454-465.

Hawken, L. C., & Horner, R. H. (2003). Evaluation of a targeted group intervention within a school-wide system of behavior support. *Journal of Behavioral Education, 12*(3), 225-240.

Irvin, L. K., Tobin, T. J., Sprague, J. R., Sugai, G., & Vincent, C. G. (2004). Validity of office discipline referral measures as indices of school-wide behavioral status and effects of school-wide behavioral interventions. *Journal of Positive Behavior Interventions, 6*(3), 131-147.

Jones, E. D., & Krouse, J. P. (1988). The effectiveness of data-based instruction by student teachers in classrooms for pupils with mild handicaps. *Teacher Education and Special Education, 11*(1), 9-19.

Moncher, F., & Prinz, R. (1991). Treatment fidelity in outcome studies. *Clinical Psychology Review, 11*, 247–266.

Noell, G. H., Duhon, G. J., Gatti, S. L., & Connell, J. E. (2002). Consultation, follow-up, and behavior management intervention implementation in general education. *School Psychology Review, 31*, 217–234.

Noell, G. H., Witt, J. C., Gilbertson, D. N., Ranier, D. D., & Freeland, J. T. (1997). Increasing teacher intervention implementation in general education settings through consultation and performance feedback. *School Psychology Quarterly, 12*, 77–88.

Noell, G. H., Witt, J. C., Slider, N. J., Connell, J. E., Gatti, S. L., & Williams, K. L., et al. (in press). Treatment implementation following behavioral consultation in schools: A comparison of three follow-up strategies. *School Psychology Review.*

Peterson, L., Homer, A., & Wonderlich, S. (1982). The integrity of independent variables in behavior analysis. *Journal of Applied Behavior Analysis, 15*, 477–492.

Salvia, J., & Ysseldyke, J. E. (2004). *Assessment in special and inclusive education* (9th ed.). Boston, MA: Houghton Mifflin.

Shapiro, E. S. (2003). *Behavior observation of students in schools* (BOSS). San Antonio, TX: Harcourt Assessment.

Sprague, J. R., Sugai, G., Horner, R. H., & Walker, H. M. (1999). Using office discipline referral data to evaluate school-wide discipline and violence prevention interventions. *Oregon School Study Council Bulletin, 42*(2).

Volpe, R. J., DiPerna, J. C., Hintze, J. M., & Shapiro, E. S. (2005). Observing students in classroom settings: A review of seven coding schemes. *School Psychology Review, 34*, 454-474.

Wickstrom, K. F., Jones, K. M., LaFleur, L.H., & Witt, J. C. (1998). An analysis of treatment integrity in school-based behavioral consultation. *School Psychology Quarterly, 13*, 141–154.

Chapter Five

Integrating Academic and Behavioral Support Practices

After reading this chapter, you will be able to:

➢ describe the impact on students' learning when combined, multi-tiered systems of academic and social-behavior support are implemented effectively;

➢ outline what a school district has to do to implement a combined behavioral and academic RTI system;

➢ define how this relates to models of student "response to intervention" for learning disabilities.

Note: This chapter is written by co-author Carol Sadler. It provides a firsthand account of the strategies and skills required to lead her district's Effective Behavior and Instructional Support (EBIS) project — a real-world example combining many of the practices and strategies described in this book.

Imagine yourself at the end of the school year and 97 percent of the kindergarten students in your district are on track for becoming readers (*see www.DIBELS.org*); over 90 percent of your third- and fifth-graders met or exceeded the state benchmarks in reading and math; the rate of office discipline referrals is less than half that of the national average for elementary schools (*see www.swis.org*); your district's middle and high school discipline referral rates are equally low in comparison to their respective national averages; and efforts are well under way to apply lessons learned from the highly successful elementary literacy model to your secondary schools (Goldman & Zinn, 2008). Using an evaluation approach centered on student response to intervention (RTI), your district is becoming a state leader — identifying students with Specific Learning Disabilities (SLD) at earlier grade levels while identification rates at higher grade levels are decreasing. To top it off, the resources you save through prevention free up resources to meet the needs of all students, including those who are struggling the most to learn (Sadler, 2007).

Those were some of the outcomes my district was experiencing when I retired in 2006. Of course, I wouldn't be talking about them if I hadn't been involved in leadership that was responsible for designing and helping to achieve them. The outcomes were the product of a systematic integration of capacity-building professional development, schoolwide positive behavior support (Sugai & Horner, 2002), early literacy, early intervention, and special education evaluation and identification using student RTI practices (Sadler & Sugai, in press). Components of the model began in 1996 with a districtwide implementation of Effective Behavior Support (EBS — a.k.a. Positive Behavior Support-PBS) (Sadler, 2000). In 2001, the district extended EBS implementation to include planning and implementation of reading/early literacy and evaluation of Specific Learning Disabilities (SLD) using RTI — based on the multi-tiered model of prevention (Walker et al., 1996). With the assistance and accountability of a model demonstration grant from U.S. Education, Office of Special Education Programs (#HB324T000025) the district's Effective Behavior and Instructional Support (EBIS) project began.

The EBIS project successfully demonstrated three outcomes for the five-year grant:

1. Sustain existing model of Effective Behavior Support in elementary schools.

2. Implement a comparable, multi-tiered model of support to improve K-3 reading outcomes.

3. Demonstrate use of RTI for Special Education evaluation and identification.

The EBIS process has four, major purposes:

1. To regularly review schoolwide academic and behavior data in order to evaluate the effectiveness of core curriculum and instructional programs;

2. To screen and identify students who are falling behind, i.e., those who need additional academic and/or behavior supports;

3. To plan, implement, modify, and evaluate the effectiveness of group and individual interventions using student performance data; and

4. To refer students for additional, special education evaluation when performance data indicates that they are not responding to well-implemented, research-based interventions at group and individual levels.

To accomplish these four purposes, the EBIS process uses four, interrelated teams of school-level administrators, teachers and staff. Collaborative, cross-program problem-solving by these teams is the heart of the work, and is continuously informed by student social-behavior and academic data. The four-team structure illustrated in Figure 1 was chosen in order to address needs at the schools for central leadership and organization, grade-level teacher collaboration, individual student support, and adequate focus on maintaining universal behavior supports.

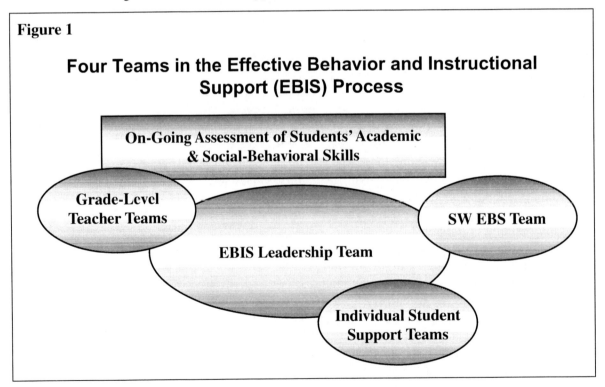

Figure 1

Four Teams in the Effective Behavior and Instructional Support (EBIS) Process

On-Going Assessment of Students' Academic & Social-Behavioral Skills

Grade-Level Teacher Teams

SW EBS Team

EBIS Leadership Team

Individual Student Support Teams

The EBIS Support Teams

Following are descriptions of the four EBIS teams. They are:

1. **Effective Behavior and Instructional Support Team (EBIS-T):** As the central leadership team, the EBIS-T is led by the principal and includes among its core members, school counselors, psychologists, and specialists from literacy/Title 1, Special Education and ELL programs. This team's purpose is to plan, implement, monitor, and maintain the effectiveness of the core academic curriculum and interventions across behavior and academic domains, with emphasis on reading as the central enabling skill. The EBIS-T reviews performance data for all students (three times/year) and monitors progress of students in small group and individual interventions (monthly or more frequently). The team is responsible for making referrals for more individualized assistance when a student is not responding to an appropriate intervention, including referral for comprehensive special education evaluation. The EBIS-T meets monthly throughout the school year.

2. **Effective Behavior Support Team (EBS-T):** Membership on this team typically includes the principal, counselor, and representative teaching, instructional and supervisory staff. This team's purpose is to plan, implement, monitor, and maintain a continuum of schoolwide and classroom behavior supports. EBS-T members meet monthly to quarterly throughout the year, depending on need. The district's EBS program has been in place for more than 10 years, so most schools have well-established routines. Table 1, next page, shows an example matrix teams use for evaluation and planning of positive behavior support activities. The matrix is organized according to the four PBS school systems: schoolwide, classroom, other settings (e.g., hallways, cafeteria, entry areas, etc.), and individual student systems. It includes questions teams should ask to evaluate their rate and level of office discipline referrals compared to typical rates and standards (*see www.swis.org*) to guide their evaluation and planning activities.

Table 1

Positive Behavior Support - Data-Based Action Planning
(Monthly Team Meetings)

FEATURES	SYSTEMS			
	Whole School	**Grade/Classroom**	**Non-Classroom**	**Individual**
Standard	80% or more students have 0-1 referrals	Less than 20% of students have 2 or more referrals. Referrals occur across grades, classrooms, settings and occasions		Few students have high numbers of referrals
Data Sources	SWIS reports, attendance reports, suspension/expulsion reports, grades/performance assessment data, individual adult concerns/reports (e.g., parents, teachers, counselors), functional assessment and behavior plan data			
Questions to Ask	What is our average number of referrals per day per month?	Are the majority of referrals coming from certain grades or classrooms? What are the major problem behaviors? Which classrooms?	Are the majority of referrals coming from specific settings/areas? What are the major problem behaviors? Which settings/areas?	How many students received 2-5 referrals? How many students received 6 or more referrals? Who are the students?
Decision Rule	If referrals >1 per day per month for every 300 students (ES) or every 100 students (MS-HS)	If >40% of referrals are coming from classrooms	If >30% of referrals are coming from a specific setting	If >20% of referrals are coming from a small group of students
Possible Actions	Re-visit schoolwide PBS program Re-teach expectations, increase/diversify acknowledgements, increase corrective feedback Implement social-behavioral curriculum (e.g., Second Steps, Steps to Respect)	Re-teach routines and expectations Provide skills groups Increase support and professional development for classroom management (teacher) Check and address student engagement during instruction Check transitions	Re-teach expectations in identified settings Increase Systematic Supervision, including acknowledgements and corrective feedback (Use Systematic Supervision Checklist) Check and correct problematic environmental features Increase structure and teaching for high-risk student groups	Check and address academic needs Implement Check In/Check Out Assign adult mentors or peer mentors Conduct functional assessment, implement behavior teaching plan Provide individualized skills instruction (academic and/or behavior) Implement 504/IEP services
Responsibility	PBS Team w/all staff	PBS Team w/appropriate staff	PBS Team w/appropriate staff	Sub-team w/appropriate staff and behavior specialist

For example, teams ask questions about their Office Discipline Referral rates, such as in column 2, at the Grade/Classroom level: "Are 40% or more of the referrals coming from classrooms?" If yes, what needs to happen? Teams may decide to put a plan in place for re-teaching routines and expectations in all, or selected, classrooms, or to increase training and support of more effective classroom management. Other options in the matrix include checking and addressing student engagement and compliance during instruction and transitions.

3. **Grade-level Teacher Teams:** Membership on these teams includes groups of teachers from each of the respective grade levels. These teacher groups meet monthly with the EBIS-T to collaborate on interventions for students needing supplemental small group or individual interventions (behaviorally as well as academically) and problem-solve program modifications based on student progress and program implementation data. The use of substitute teachers who "float" into the grade levels and release the teachers for these meetings is the preferred method.

4. **Individual Student Support Team (ISS-T):** Membership on this team varies depending on the student of concern. The team will typically include the student's teacher, special education specialist, counselor, school psychologist and/or others with expertise in diagnostic teaching, data utilization, problem-solving, functional assessment, behavior intervention planning, and special education evaluation. Parents are invited to attend ISS-T meetings regarding their child, and are kept closely advised of their child's program and progress by the classroom teacher or ISS plan manager, a position that is assigned by the team upon developing each student's individual action plan. The purpose of the ISS-T is to continue evaluation of the student's response to intervention by individualizing and intensifying interventions when a student has not responded to small group interventions, and then more closely monitoring the student's program and progress. Most of the students served by the ISS-T will have come through the small group phase of the EBIS process, thus will have failed to respond to at least two, prior interventions. A few students also may be referred to the ISS-T because they present extreme behavioral challenges. Thus, the ISS-T's role can be similar to the role of the "Action Team" in the schoolwide PBS model. Both models acknowledge that although the major focus is prevention, it is important to build in capacity to respond quickly to intense and immediate individual student or teacher needs.

Figure 2, next page, illustrates the flow of EBIS teamwork through four basic phases. Phases are used as a framework for explaining the process and should not be interpreted as isolated steps. In fact, a student may move up and down, or in or out, of the phases during the course of an instruction/intervention cycle. This flowchart was adapted from a version called "Daisy" created by the Tigard-Tualatin Learning Disabilities Task Force, September 2001.

Figure 2: The Flow of EBIS Teamwork through Four Phases: Universal screening, target groups interventions, intensified/individualized interventions, and referral for special education evaluation

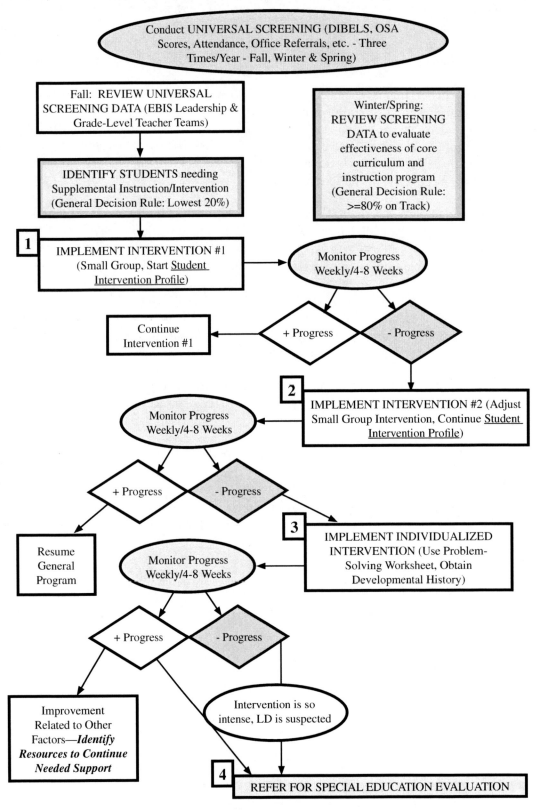

Phase 1 – Screening for Core Planning

Three times each year, starting in September, EBIS leadership and grade-level teacher teams gather to review screening and other data on student performance, including all available academic and behavior information (e.g., Dynamic Indicators of Basic Early Literacy Skills (DIBELS- Good & Kaminski, 1996), other curriculum-based measures, Oregon state assessments, attendance, office referrals, grades, teacher or parent concerns, etc.). These screening meetings have two functions, as referenced earlier: (1) to check on the effectiveness of core instruction (informally known as the "80% rule"), and (2) to identify students who are not responding adequately to core instruction, and who, therefore, need supplemental intervention (informally known as the "20% group"). Prevention logic suggesting that the core can be expected to maintain 80 percent or more students on track for benchmarks (Walker et al., 1996) works well for general, positive behavior support but may not set a high-enough standard when it comes to reading, especially at the early grades. Good (2007), for example, notes that for kindergarten, an effective core curriculum should support 95 percent or more students to stay on track for reading benchmarks. The use of rules for making broad decisions about allocating resources should not be confused with or serve as a substitute for setting and using high standards or goals for student achievement.

Phase 2 – Screening for Supplemental Intervention

In the K-5 EBIS process, all students who are performing in the intensive and low-strategic ranges on the DIBELS (Good & Kaminski, 1996) (or comparable ranges on other curriculum-based reading measures) are listed on the EBIS Group Intervention Planning Form (Figure 3, next page) (*see also www.ttsd.k12.or.us*). Team members sometimes add additional students for whom they have concerns at these meetings, and, depending on their available resources, schools may have to use a "triage" process to prioritize students for interventions.

Figure 3

EBIS GROUP INTERVENTIONS & PLANNING FORM

School: **Date:**

Last Name	First Name	Grade	Homeroom Teacher	Behav/Social/Emot	Attendance	Tardies	Reading	Writing	Math	Health/Physical	DIBELS ISF Raw Score	DIBELS/IDEL PSF Raw Score	DIBELS/IDEL NWF RawScore	DIBELS/IDEL ORF(Median Score)	CBM-Other Score	Reading RIT Score	Math RIT Score	Test Window: F(1), W(2),and/or S(3)	Interventions

Issues — Code "1" for "YES" | *Enter Scores*

The EBIS leadership and teacher teams brainstorm new and/or identify available interventions, arrange students in small groups by instructional need and level of intensity (e.g., fluency practice, intensive level), and agree on implementation plans. The district's current standard protocols of interventions at Tiers I, II and III, for K-5 reading and K-12 behavior, are provided in Figures 4 and 5, next pages. These protocols are used exclusively by the district with extensive training and support for implementation and fidelity. Classroom teachers share in providing small group interventions, but the bulk of the interventions are taught by instructional assistants with monitoring and support by the teachers and literacy specialists. The classroom teachers are responsible for keeping parents informed of their child's program and progress at this phase of the EBIS process.

Figure 4

Tigard-Tualatin Standard Reading Protocol, K-5

GRADE	TIER I: PRIMARY Time	PROGRAM OPTIONS	TIER II: STRATEGIC Time & Group Size	PROGRAM OPTIONS	TIER III: INTENSIVE Time and Group Size	PROGRAM OPTIONS
K	60 minutes daily	Macmillan Macmillan & Fast Track SFA	Add 10 minutes daily Large group	*Ladders to Literacy *PA in Young Children *Road to the Code *Earobics *Daisy Castle	Add 30 minutes daily Small group	*ERI only for 30 mins. OR *Language for Learning and ERI for 45 minutes *Fast Track Phonics
1	90 minutes daily	Macmillan SFA	Add 30 minutes daily Small group	*Triumphs *SFA Tutoring	Add 30 minutes Small group	*ERI only for 30 mins. OR *Language for Learning and ERI for 45 minutes *Fast Track Phonics *Reading Mastery
2	90 minutes daily	Macmillan Reading Mastery	Add 30 minutes daily Small group	*Phonics For Reading *Read Naturally *STARS	Add 30-45 minutes of intervention daily If CORE is reduced to 30 minutes (vocab/comp) then add a minimum of two 30-45 minute intervention periods daily as determined by progress Small group	*Triumphs *Reading Mastery *Read Naturally *Language for Thinking (w/ reading intervention) * Horizons

continues

continued

3	90 minutes daily	**Macmillan** **Reading Mastery**	**Add 30 minutes daily** Small group	*Phonics For Reading *Read Naturally *STARS *Connections for Comp. *Reading Success	ADD 30-45 minutes of intervention daily If CORE is reduced to 30 minutes (vocab/comp) then add a minimum of two 30-45 minute intervention periods daily as determined by progress Small group	*Triumphs *Horizons *Read Naturally *Reading Mastery *Reading Success
4-5	90 minutes daily	**Macmillan** **Reading Mastery**	**Add 15-30 minutes daily** Small group	*REWARDS *Phonics For Reading *Six-Minute Solution *Read Naturally *Collaborative Strategic Reading *STARS *Connections for Comp. *Reading Success	ADD 30-45 minutes of intervention daily If CORE is reduced to 30 minutes (vocab/comp) then add a minimum of two 30-45 minute intervention periods daily as determined by progress Small group	*Triumphs *Reading Mastery *Read Naturally *Great Leaps *Corrective Reading *Reading Success *Horizons

Reprinted with permission from the Tigard-Tualatin School District, Tigard, Ore. All rights reserved.

Figure 5

Tigard-Tualatin Standard Behavior Protocol, K-12

Grade Level(s)	Universal Screening Tools	Core Program	Second-Tier Interventions	Third-Tier Interventions
K-1	• First Step To Success Behavior Screener • Phoneme Segmentation Fluency • Office Discipline Referrals • Attendance Reports • Suspension/Expulsion Data	• School Rules & Behavior Expectations Are Explicitly Taught to <u>ALL</u> Students • All Students Regularly & Consistently Acknowledged for Demonstrating Behavior Expectations	• Re-Teach Expectations • Check & Connect Programs • Adult Mentoring • Skills Groups • Behavior Contracts • *Targeted* Social/Emotional Curriculum <u>Follow-up</u> (e.g., Second Steps with Small Group of Struggling Students)	• Core + Second Tier **and…** • First Step To Success • Functional Behavior Assessment & Individual Behavior Support Plans • Individualized Behavior Goals and Progress Monitoring (IEP & 504)
2-12	• Office Discipline Referrals • Attendance Reports • Suspension/Expulsion Data • Oregon Healthy Teens Survey • Social Marketing Surveys	• All Students Immediately & Reliably Corrected When Behavior Expectations Are Not Demonstrated. Positive Behavior Expectation Re-taught & Reinforced Immediately • Schoolwide Social/Emotional Curriculum Delivery (e.g., Second Steps, Steps to Respect, etc.)	• Re-Teach Expectations • Check & Connect • Strategic "Positive Referrals" for Identified Students Working Toward Increased Positive Behavior • Adult Mentoring • Peer Mentoring • Skills Groups • Behavior Contracts • Advisory Classes • *Targeted* Social/Emotional Curriculum <u>Follow-up</u> (e.g., Second Steps with Small Group of Struggling Students)	• Core + Second Tier **and…** • Functional Behavior Assessment & Individual Behavior Support Plans • Individualized Behavior Goals and Progress Monitoring (IEP & 504)
Who does this work?	EBIS / EBS Teams FSTS Staff	ALL STAFF	Appropriate Staff as Determined by EBS Team	Appropriate Staff as Determined by EBS Team

continues

continued

Decision Rules:

- Screening
  - K-1
    - Every student that a K-1 teacher or staff member believes will need behavior support is screened with the First Step to Success Screener.
    - Students who score in the "high-risk" or "extreme risk" range on the First Step to Success (FSTS) screener are considered for participation in the FSTS program.
    - Students identified as "at risk" or "deficit" on Phoneme Segmentation Fluency (PSF) on the DIBELS are considered for Second Tier Reading &/or Behavior Interventions.
    - **Students who are identified as "at risk" or "deficit" on the PSF AND "extreme risk" on the FSTS screener MUST be discussed by the EBIS team for possible referral to the First Step to Success Program.**

  - K-5
    - Office Discipline Referral Data reviewed monthly. If more than 1 referral per day per month for every 250 students, revisit the CORE and look for patterns in location, time, grade, type, and frequency of incidents.

  - 6-12
    - Office Discipline Referral Data reviewed monthly. If more than 1 referral per day per month for every 200 students, revisit the CORE and look for patterns in location, time, grade, type, and frequency of incidents.

  - K-12
    - If more than 20% of all students received 2 or more referrals: revisit the CORE.
    - More than 30% of referrals occur in a specific area of the school: re-teach specific common area behavior expectations, acknowledge/reward positive behavior, & correct inappropriate behavior immediately.
    - More than 40% of referrals occur in classrooms: re-teach classroom expectations, increase professional development in classroom management strategies, and/or revisit CORE instruction in specific classrooms.

- Progress monitoring:
  - K/1: 1x/week PSF & Behavior Intervention Data.
  - K-12: Behavior data from Check & Connect programs.
  - K-12: More than 5 absences, or more than 3 counseling or discipline referrals, in a 30-day period.
  - K-12: Progress on individual behavior goals or Behavior Support Plan.

- Intensifying intervention:
  - Students who receive 2 – 5 referrals should receive CORE + Second Tier Interventions.
  - If progress is below the expected rate after 6 to 8 weeks of Second Tier Intervention, students move to Third Tier Interventions (consider performing a Functional Behavior Assessment and developing a Behavior Support Plan).
  - Students receiving 6 or more behavior referrals: perform an appropriate Functional Behavior Assessment & develop a Behavior Support Plan.

Reprinted with permission from the Tigard-Tualatin School District, Tigard, Ore. All rights reserved.

After the initial teamwork in the fall on identifying and grouping students for supplemental interventions, the EBIS leadership team and grade-level teachers meet monthly to review progress data on all students in supplemental interventions. The monthly meetings are brisk, lasting from 45 minutes to an hour for each grade level. Student successes are celebrated quickly followed by problem-solving for students not making progress, and deciding on adjustments to their interventions that will be tested over the next month. For each student in an intervention process, one of three decisions is made at each review:

1. The student's progress is satisfactory, therefore, the supplemental, small group intervention is no longer necessary (the student may return to core instruction alone);

2. the supplemental, small group intervention appears to be working and should be continued as is for an additional period of time (usually at least a month); or

3. the supplemental, small group intervention is not working and should be revised.

If the team's decision is to revise or refine the current intervention, a checklist, Options for Changes in Interventions (Figure 6, next page) is used to identify and document changes. At this point, problem-solving emphasizes efficiency (what is the smallest change we can make that will have the greatest effect?) within the more research-minded goal of being able to link student response, or lack of it, to a particular intervention change.

Additionally, at this phase, teams begin to keep track of intervention details using the Student Intervention Profile (Figure 7, page 106). The district has part- to full-time Literacy/Title I specialists and full-time counselors at each elementary school. The literacy specialists typically maintain documentation on students in reading interventions, and the school counselors maintain documentation on students in behavior interventions.

Figure 6

EBIS Options for Changes in Interventions

Student:_____ Date:_____

Options for the Student
- ❑ Increase Motivation
  - ○ Add incentives
  - ○ Change incentives
  - ○ Adjust behavior plan
  - ○ Increase success level

- ❑ Increase active engagement
  - ○ Number of responses per session
  - ○ Teach, review and post standards of behavior

- ❑ Increase regular attendance
- ❑ Ensure student skill level matches instruction
  - ○ Skill grouping
  - ○ Differentiated instruction

- ❑ Increase types of cueing approaches
  - ○ Visual
  - ○ Auditory
  - ○ Tactile

Options for Curriculum/Program
- ❑ Check fidelity of implementation of program
  - ○ Provide additional training
  - ○ Add a coaching component

- ❑ Add another component using
  - ○ Existing program
  - ○ Another part of a program to reinforce a skill
  - ○ The computer

- ❑ Move to a more structured intervention program
- ❑ Change the core program

Options for Instruction (Practices)
- ❑ Skill Grouping/Differentiated Instruction
- ❑ Increase pace of instruction
- ❑ Increase opportunities to respond
- ❑ Employ standard cueing correction procedures
- ❑ Pre-teach concepts outside the group
- ❑ Build/activate prior knowledge

Options for Instruction (Logistics)
- ❑ Reduce size of instructional group
- ❑ Add additional instruction time
  - ○ Double dosing
  - ○ Different materials
- ❑ Change instructor
- ❑ Change seating within group
- ❑ Provide instruction in small units throughout the day
- ❑ Change physical environment

Figure 7

EBIS Student Intervention Profile

Student Name: _____   *ID Number:* _____

Initial Data Information

Initial Grade Level: _____

Date: _____

DIBELS/CBM Scores: ISF _____   PSF _____   NWF _____   ORF (Median) _____

Reading RIT Score: _____

Math RIT Score: _____

Writing Scores: _____

Attendance Issues: _____

Behavioral Issues: _____

Intervention #1   Classroom: ____ Title 1: ____ ELL: ____ EBIS Grant: ____ Other: _____

Start Date: _____ Current Grade Level: _____

Curriculum: _____

Group Size:	Individual: ____ 2-5: ____ 6-15: ____ 15-30: ____ Class: ____
Frequency:	One/Wk: ____ Two/Wk: ____ Three/Wk: ____ Four/Wk: ____ Daily: ____
Duration:	15 min.: ___ 20 min.: ____ 30 min.: ____ 45 min.: ____ 60 min.: ____ Other: ___
Intervention Teacher:	License Reg: ___ License Sp.: ____ IA: ____ Counselor: ____ Volunteer: ____

End Date: _____   **Progress Data:**

Intervention #2   Classroom: ____ Title 1: ____ ELL: ____ EBIS Grant: ____ Other: _____

Start Date: _____ Current Grade Level: _____

Curriculum: _____

Group Size:	Individual: ____ 2-5: ____ 6-15: ____ 15-30: ____ Class: ____
Frequency:	One/Wk: ____ Two/Wk: ____ Three/Wk: ____ Four/Wk: ____ Daily: ____
Duration:	15 min.: ___ 20 min.: ___ 30 min.: ___ 45 min.: ___ 60 min.: ___ Other: ___
Intervention Teacher:	License Reg: ___ License Sp.: ____ IA: ____ Counselor: ____ Volunteer: ____

End Date: _____   **Progress Data:**

Intervention #3   Classroom: ____ Title 1: ____ ELL: ____ EBIS Grant: ____ Other: _____

Start Date: _____ Current Grade Level: _____

Curriculum: _____

Group Size:	Individual: ____ 2-5: ____ 6-15: ____ 15-30: ____ Class: ____
Frequency:	One/Wk: ____ Two/Wk: ____ Three/Wk: ____ Four/Wk: ____ Daily: ____
Duration:	15 min.: ___ 20 min.: ____ 30 min.: ____ 45 min.: ____ 60 min.: ____ Other: ___
Intervention Teacher:	License Reg: ___ License Sp.: ____ IA: ____ Counselor: ____ Volunteer: ____

End Date: _____   **Progress Data:**

Figure 8 provides an example of EBIS decision rules for grades 1-5, illustrating selection rules for identifying students, and guidelines for monitoring progress and intensifying interventions.

Figure 8

Decision Rules for the EBIS Process, Grades 1-5

Place students in the 20% group when:

- Academic skills fall below benchmark and place them in the lowest 20% compared to their peers on one or more of the following measures: DIBELS, DIBELS-ORF, Math & Writing curriculum-based assessments, Oregon State Assessments.

- Chronic problems with attendance and/or socio-emotional-behavioral skills occur, as defined by:

  - More than 5 absences in a 30-day period

  - 3 or more discipline or counseling referrals in a 30-day period

Modify interventions when:

- Progress monitoring indicates 3 or more data points below the aimline.

  - If data is highly variable, maintain the current intervention for another month to establish a trendline.

    o Progress is monitored once weekly

Individualize interventions when:

- Progress trend under small group instruction is below the aimline for two consecutive intervention periods (at 8, 12 or 16 weeks, depending on the data).

Refer to Special Education when:

- After one highly structured, individualized intervention, progress continues below aimline.

    o Progress is monitored twice weekly or more frequently if needed

---

Phase 3 – Individualized Intervention

The general decision rule is that if after two (2) small group interventions, each lasting four to eight weeks in duration (an arbitrary, but practical "decision rule"), teams determine that a student is "not" responding adequately and is unlikely to do so without an additional modification to the current intervention, the student is referred for an individually designed intervention (not necessarily one-to-one, we should add). It is important to note that teams are making their judgments about student "response" by comparing a student's progress under a certain intervention to the progress of peers receiving similar interventions, and to overall, grade-level standards for that particular student's age or grade. (For information on the technical details of this approach, see Fuchs & Fuchs, 1998, description of "treatment validity" and "dual discrepancy".)

When a student is referred for this "individualizing" phase of the EBIS process, parents are informed and invited to attend the evaluation and planning meeting. A developmental history is obtained from the parents via interview (often by the school psychologist) regardless of whether the parent is able to attend the meeting.

The individualizing phase of the EBIS process conforms to the following protocol:

> An Individual Student Support Team (ISS-T) is convened and conducts a comprehensive school records review using the *Individual Problem Solving Worksheet*. This worksheet was designed by the Learning Disabilities Task Force (September, 2001) and is available at the district's Web site, given earlier. The worksheet guides teams to summarize the student's attendance and academic history in reading, math, and written language. Prompts on the worksheet help team members address potential, alternate explanations for a student's lack of progress. These alternate explanations are equivalent to the "exclusionary criteria" that must be considered when conducting an evaluation for Specific Learning Disabilities (SLD). That is, a student may not be found SLD if his/her difficulties appear to be primarily due to: (i) visual, hearing or motor disability, (ii) mental retardation, (iii) emotional disturbance, (iv) cultural factors, (v) environmental or economic disadvantage, or (vi) limited English proficiency.

On reviewing information from the individual problem-solving worksheet and related information, the team develops an individual student action plan. At this phase, an EBIS-ISS-T case manager is assigned (not to be confused with special education case manager role). The case manager's responsibilities include:

- monitoring implementation of the student's action plan, according to the schedule agreed upon by the team;

- checking and ensuring fidelity of implementation;

- assuming responsibility for tracking intervention details by continuing the Student Intervention Profile;

- assisting the teacher to maintain communications with the parent(s); and

- reporting to the EBIS Leadership Team on the student's progress, and making recommendations for further intervention or evaluation.

The "individualizing" phase of the EBIS process continues for four to eight weeks, depending on student progress and team judgment.

It is important to note that if the team believes that the student's intervention profile signals a possible emotional disturbance (ED), assessment procedures shift to include the required components for ED evaluation. In this particular district, ED evaluations have been guided by long-standing state technical recommendations for a period of six to eight weeks of "pre-referral intervention" prior to individual, psychological testing for ED, to rule out potential instruction-related problems associated with the general education environment before considering special education. Thus, the district's ED evaluations were "RTI-like" well prior to implementation of EBIS. That said, the district's primary emphasis for EBIS was on applying RTI practices for SLD evaluation over that of ED evaluation. Additional training and support through the EBIS project and special education department focused on improving functional assessment and behavior instructional planning skills of staff in both general and special education, but the development of a new and improved ED evaluation approach, originally envisioned in the EBIS grant, was not accomplished.

The four phases of the EBIS process are included in Table 2, next page. The phases show the progression that occurs from schoolwide assessment and prevention systems to additional, but minimal, assessment and targeted, small group, "standard protocol" interventions to intensive assessment and individualized interventions. Examples of interventions and progress monitoring data are provided, as well as suggested monitoring frequency at each phase.

In the first phase of EBIS, core programs, available to all students, include schoolwide behavior instruction, and classroom and grade-level behavior and academic supports. Selected core programs are the best available, research-supported examples, and, consequently, are expected to work for the majority (80 percent to 90 percent) of students. For some students, response will improve when a relatively small amount of extra attention and instruction is provided at classroom and grade levels.

At the second phase, small group, standard interventions implemented by support staff are added to the core curriculum and teacher-driven, grade-level efforts. On the behavior side, a typical standard intervention is "Check In/Check Out" (Sinclair, Christenson, Evelo, & Hurley, 1998). It is resource-efficient, requiring less staff ingenuity and time, and known to be effective for students who are positively reinforced by adult attention (as many as 80 percent of students with compliance problems in school). On the academic side, the Early Reading Intervention (Kame'enui & Simmons, 1998-2003) is used extensively in the district to teach phonemic awareness skills to K-1 students with intensive-level deficits (see standard reading protocol, Tier III, Grades K-1, in Figure 4, *supra*).

Table 2

EBIS Process Phases, Example Interventions and Progress Monitoring Measures and Frequency

EBIS PROCESS PHASE	EXAMPLE INTERVENTION	PROGRESS MEASURE	FREQUENCY
EBIS Phase 1 Universal Screening, effective schoolwide behavior and academic systems Grade-level teacher collaboration and alignment	PBS Core Features: rules, explicit teaching, systems for acknowledging and correcting, team- and data-based decision-making; Second Step (Committee for Children) Research-based Core Academic Curricula and effective classroom instruction	Office discipline referrals, schoolwide PBS implementation data, classroom or program progress data, classroom products, grades	Three times/yr. (fall, winter & spring)
EBIS Phase 2 Identification of students for supplemental intervention, implementation of standard protocol interventions, collaboration of grade level and EBIS leadership teams	Check-In/Check Out, Adult/ Student Mentoring, Behavior and Academic Skills Groups	Program Progress/ Skills Group Data, Counselor/ Mentor Reports Grades	Monthly to Weekly
EBIS Phase 3 Referral to Individual Student Support Team (ISS-T), additional information-gathering, implementation of individualized intervention	Behavior Support Plans, Home-School Contracts, First Step to Success (Walker et al., 1998). Additional function-based behavior and targeted academic support	Program Progress/ Skills Group Data, Teacher / Parent Reports	Twice Weekly to Daily
EBIS Phase 4 Referral for continuation and completion of Special Education Evaluation	Continuation of intensive, individualized academic and behavior support, mental health, family support (wrap-around) services	Program Progress/ Skills Group Data, Teacher / Parent / Counseling/ Health/ Mental Health Reports	Daily

At the third phase, in order to develop a more intensive, individualized intervention, information on the student's academic skills, and school and developmental history are routinely collected, as described earlier. Functional behavior assessments are conducted, as well, when behavior problems indicate the need. Some standard protocol interventions are used at this phase also, such as the more resource intensive, but highly effective, First Steps to Success (FSTS) program (Walker et al., 1998) in which behavior modification, coaching, and parent training strategies combine to reverse antisocial behaviors and increase academic engagement of K-1 students.

While responsibility for planning and implementing individualized interventions is still conceptualized as a general education responsibility in the EBIS model, comprehensive, functional assessment and behavior intervention planning, in particular, may be better accomplished as a part of a more formal, diagnostic, special education process, given the high level of expertise, time, and resources such individualized and intensive behavior supports require (Crone & Horner, 2003; O'Neill et al., 1997). In such case as is true for implementation of FSTS, parent permission is required. At Phase 4, if it has not already occurred, responsibility for intervention is formally transferred from general to special education for completion of the evaluation process.

As a final comment, district and school leaders with whom the authors have worked have identified critical features associated with leadership and sustainability of RTI practices, such as those implemented by the district highlighted in this chapter. Mellard and Johnson (2008, p. 135) describe a strong RTI process as including the following critical features:

- High-quality, scientifically based classroom instruction

- Schoolwide screening of academics and behavior

- Progress monitoring of student performance

- Implementation of appropriate, research-based interventions at all tiers

- Fidelity checks on implementation

The readiness assessment provided in Chapter 1 of this book provides a good starting place to examine your district's implementation in relation to these essential RTI features, along with the foundations that need to be addressed when embarking on any substantial educational change — your agreements and commitments regarding vision, goals, and leadership.

References

Committee for Children, Seattle, Washington. *Second Step* and *Steps to Respect* curricula.

Crone, D. A., & Horner, R. H. (2003). *Building positive behavior support systems in schools: Functional behavioral assessment.* New York: Guilford Press.

Fuchs, L., & Fuchs, D. (1998). Treatment validity: A unifying concept for reconceptualizing the identification of learning disabilities. *Learning Disabilities Research & Practice, 13*(4), 204-219.

Good, R. H., & Kaminski, R. A. (1996). Assessment for instructional decisions: Toward a proactive/prevention model of decision making for early literacy skills. *School Psychology Quarterly, 11,* 326-336.

Good, R. H. (2007). *Using data to guide instruction for all learners.* Presentation at State Department of Education School Leadership Conference, 7 November 2007. Baltimore, MD.

Goldman, D., & Zinn, P. (2008). *Secondary EBIS: A district & classroom perspective on a systemic secondary reading program.* Presentation at the Oregon Positive Behavior Supports Conference, 12 March 2008.

Kame'enui, E., & Simmons, D. (1998-2003). Project OPTIMIZE (U.S. Department of Education, #H023C80156).

McIntosh, K., Horner, R. H., Chard, D. J., Boland, J. B., & Good III, R. H. (2006). The use of reading and behavior screening measures to predict nonresponse to school-wide positive behavior support: A longitudinal analysis. *School Psychology Review, 35*(2), 275-291.

McIntosh, K., & Sadler, C. (n.d.). *The relation between early reading skills and problem behavior: Replication and further analyses.* Manuscript in process.

Mellard, D. F., & Johnson, E. (2008). *RTI: A practitioner's guide to implementing response to intervention.* CA: Corwin Press.

O'Neill, R. E., Horner, R. H., Albin, R. W., Sprague, J. R., Newton, S., & Storey, K. (1997). *Functional assessment and program development for problem behavior: A practical handbook.* (Second ed.). Pacific Grove, CA: Brookes/Cole Publishing.

Sadler, C. (2000). Effective behavior support implementation at the district level: Tigard-Tualatin School District. *Journal of Positive Behavior Interventions 2*(4), 241-243.

Sadler, C. (2007). *Effective behavior and instructional support (Combining PBS, EIS, and RTI).* Presentations at OSEP Part B Regulations Regional Implementation Meetings, 12-13, 15-16 February 2007. Los Angeles, CA and Kansas City, MS.

Sadler, C., & Sugai. G. (2008). Effective behavior and instructional support: A district model for early identification and prevention of reading and behavior problems. *Journal of Positive Behavior Interventions & Supports* (in press).

Sinclair, M. F., Christenson, S. L., Evelo, D. L., & Hurley, C. M. (1998). Dropout prevention for youth with disabilities: Efficacy of a sustained school engagement procedure. *Exceptional Children, 65*(1), 7-21.

Sugai, G., & Horner, R. (2002). The evolution of discipline practices: School-wide positive behavior support. *Child and Family Behavior Therapy, 24*, 23-50.

Walker, H. M., Horner, R. H., Sugai, G., Bullis, M., Sprague, J. R., & Bricker, D. (1996). Integrated approaches to preventing antisocial behavior patterns among school-age children and youth. *Journal of Emotional & Behavioral Disorders, 4*(4), 194-209.

Walker, H. M., Kavanagh, K., Stiller, B., Golly, A., Severson, H. H., & Feil, E. G. (1998). First Step to Success: An early intervention approach for preventing school antisocial behavior. *Journal of Emotional and Behavioral Disorders, 6*(2), 66-80.

Chapter Six

The Relationship Between Special Education Law and Behavioral RTI Practices

After reading this chapter, you will be able to:

➤ describe how FAPE can be related to the provision of behavior supports;

➤ define the relationship between related services and supplementary aids and services and RTI decision-making when the student exhibits problem behavior;

➤ discuss the IDEA intention for how the IEP team should address behavior using multiple tiers of support;

➤ describe behavioral progress monitoring and goal development for students with IEPs;

➤ discuss the relationship between behavioral interventions and discipline procedures, and how that relates to a school's responsive RTI structure.

Overview of IDEA 2004 and the RTI Logic for Students with IEPs

Behavioral RTI is a systematic approach to providing increasing services and supports to reduce the negative effects of problem behavior on academic and social emotional functioning. That is, behavioral RTI is much more than just a process to determine eligibility for special education. The logic and procedures of RTI also are required once eligibility has been determined. An individualized education program (IEP) is essentially a document that outlines what constitutes a free appropriate public education (FAPE) for a student who has met the two-pronged test: (1) The student has one of the 13 federal disabilities, and (2) the student is in need of special education due to the unique nature of that disability. Figure 1, next page, illustrates the 13 eligibility categories under the Individuals with Disabilities Education Act (IDEA).

Figure 1

13 IDEA Eligibility Categories

1. autism (34 CFR 300.8(c)(1))

2. deaf-blindness (34 CFR 300.8(c)(2))

3. deafness (34 CFR 300.8(c)(3))

4. emotional disturbance (34 CFR 300.8(c)(4))

5. hearing impairments (34 CFR 300.8(c)(5))

6. mental retardation (34 CFR 300.8(c)(6))

7. multiple disabilities (34 CFR 300.8(c)(7))

8. orthopedic impairments (34 CFR 300.8(c)(8))

9. other health impairment (34 CFR 300.8(c)(9))

10. specific learning disability (34 CFR 300.8(c)(10))

11. speech or language impairments (34 CFR 300.8(c)(11))

12. traumatic brain injury (34 CFR 300.8(c)(12))

13. visual impairment including blindness (34 CFR 300.8(c)(13))

(IDEA 2004 also permits states to identify a 14th category for students from ages 3 through 9 who are "developmentally delayed." This designation can apply to "any subset of that age range, including ages 3 through 5." 34 CFR 300.8(b).)

Special Education

Special education is defined in IDEA regulation 34 CFR 300.39 as "specially designed instruction," at no cost to the parents, intended to meet the unique needs of a child with a disability. Special education is not limited to a typical school environment and must be provided in a variety of other settings, such as institutions and hospitals (34 CFR 300.39(a)(1)), to the extent necessary to provide FAPE. "Specially designed instruction" means adapting, as appropriate to the needs of an eligible child under Part B, the content, methodology, or delivery of instruction: (i) to address the unique needs of the child that result from the child's disability, and (ii) to ensure access of the child to the general curriculum, so that he or she can meet the educational standards within the jurisdiction of the public agency that apply to all children. 34 CFR 300.39(b)(3).

An evaluation, as described in 34 CFR 300.301-300.306, will have been completed to determine if the student needs special education and related services as a result of his disability or disabilities. Everything we provide, which must be in the least restrictive environment, must allow this FAPE to be attained for this student, providing "some educational benefit" for the student through our IEP process so that educational standards are met. Some educational benefit is beyond minimal benefit, but short of maximum benefit according to the U.S. Supreme Court's decision in *Board of Education of Hendrick Hudson Central School District v. Rowley*, 553 IDELR 656 (EHLR 553:656) (U.S. 1982).

Once the student has an IEP, at each IEP team meeting, members must address, under special factors, whether or not the student has a behavior impeding his or her learning or that of peers. In other words, the intent of the law is that if behavior is a variable interfering with academic success, this must be addressed by the IEP team just as a disability interfering with academic success must be addressed in the IEP so that FAPE is achieved. Once the team believes the behavior is interfering with learning, specifically identifying which positive behavioral interventions, strategies and supports will be used to address the problem must be a part of the IEP. Figure 2, next page, illustrates these concepts about behavior. This chart summarizes how IDEA 1997 and the 2004 reauthorized IDEA have conceptual underpinnings that are different from earlier perspectives on behavior present in school practices. Figure 3, page 119, provides a simple list of behavioral terminology that links law with applied behavior analysis, the paradigm that is the underpinning of IDEA and response to behavior.

Figure 2

IDEA Conceptual Underpinnings: Shifting Our Understanding of Behavior

CURRENT THINKING	PAST PRACTICE	THE DIFFERENCE
Students may require *"Behavior Support"*— *To address what we can do to proactively prevent behavior problems and support desired behaviors*	Students may require *"Behavior Management"* — *To address what we can do to manage the problem once it has occurred*	*"Behavior Support"* implies addressing Environment, Teaching Strategies, Teaching New Behaviors, and Using Positive Reinforcement Strategies.
		"Behavior Management" came to imply focusing on consequences, whether positive or negative.
Behavior Support Plans should focus on understanding "why" the behavior occurred (i.e., the "function" or "communicative intent") then proceed to focus on teaching/eliciting an alternative behavior that meets the student's needs in alternative, more acceptable ways.	*Behavior Management Plans* came to imply focusing on specifying the consequences of misbehavior, and to some extent, the consequences of acceptable behavior (i.e., the absence of the problem behavior).	*Past practice* rarely attempted to understand the reasons a maladaptive behavior occurred.
		Current practice, by understanding the behavior and teaching alternatives or changing environmental conditions, plans to seek permanent change through assuring needs are met.
Antecedents (the immediate and immediate past "triggers" or "predictors" for the behavior) are critical in changing behavior. *Focus:* What we can actively do (e.g., teach, structure the environment) to change the behavior?	*Consequences* were attempted to be made so compelling that the student would stop a behavior (i.e., either so strongly aversive that the student didn't want to choose the maladaptive behavior or so strongly positive that the student avoided the problem behavior to get the reinforcer). *Focus:* What the student must do to avoid our punishment or get something we provide if the problem disappears.	*Consequence-based Plans:* For many students, neither a strong enough punishment, nor a strong enough reinforcer can be found to change the behavior.
		Antecedent-based Plans: Can result in changing environmental conditions (e.g., time, space, materials, interactions), and student skills so that lasting change is possible.
Philosophy: Positive behavior needs to be taught (i.e., modeled, shaped, cued in a conducive environment).	*Philosophy:* Problem behavior needs to be controlled or eliminated. Positive behaviors are to be expected regardless of environment.	*Controlling Behavior:* Becoming increasing more difficult in today's classrooms.
		Teaching Behavior: Has potential for lasting change.

Figure 3

Guide to Behavior Terminology

DIANA BROWNING WRIGHT*

*This chart is abridged and altered from a California-specific chart originally authored by Diana Browning Wright, PENT Director (California's Positive Environments, Network of Trainers) with input from Joan Justice Brown & Kimble Morton, PENT Leaders, 2008. The California version is located at: *www.pent.ca.gov*

Term	Definition	Law/ Best Practice	When Required
Functional Behavioral Assessment **FBA**	An evidence-based, analytical process based on observations, review of records, interviews and data analysis. It strives to determine the immediate and immediate past antecedents and consequences supporting the problem behavior. This assessment is the first step in designing function-based interventions that promote educational success. FBA is necessary prior to identifying a functionally equivalent replacement behavior. The function of a behavior will be to either 1. get something or 2. reject something. **Remember:** Even if the behavior is determined to not be a manifestation of the disability, other sections of Federal law/ Regs require consideration of whether this behavior impedes the learning of the student or peers, with required positive behavioral intervention strategies and supports (likely to be a BSP). If behavior results in multiple suspensions, this IS behavior impeding the learning of the student or peers and should trigger addressing the behavior.	**Law:** FBA is required in IDEA 2004 and Federal Regulations in a disciplinary context for students with IEPs, when the behavior has been determined to be a Manifestation of the Disability. This occurs under two conditions. See: 34 C.F.R Section 300.536 and right column. See forms that support this process: *www.pent.ca.gov/ 10Forms/suspensionbeyond. doc & www.pent.ca.gov/10Forms/sus-pensionpast.doc & www.pent. ca.gov/10Forms/mandetanaly-sis.doc* Federal law requires the implementation of a behavioral intervention plan (usually termed Behavior Support Plan in California) whenever it requires an FBA. See: *www.pent. ca.gov/forms* **Best Practice:** All behavior plans should be based on why the behavior occurs, i.e., the function it serves for the student. The degree of data necessary to support conclusions should increase with the severity of the problem.	Two instances trigger a Manifestation Determination and possible FBA (A signed assessment plan is required if FBA conducted): **1. Consecutive suspensions past 10 days**, i.e., on the 11th day in a row, services must be provided AND an MD is required. (Often a student will exceed 10 days awaiting expulsion proceedings). If this misbehavior is determined to be an MD an FBA is required, otherwise it is not required following the manifestation determination. **2. Cumulative suspensions past 10 days in a school year:** Principal or other responsible person is required to determine if this series of removals constitutes a pattern resulting in a de facto **change in placement** because: 1. 10 days were exceeded; 2.This misconduct is substantially similar to previous behaviors; and 3. Other factors such as length of each removal, proximity of removals and total amount of time of cumulative removals suggests this suspension is subjecting the student to a change in placement. If it is concluded that this suspension DOES constitute a pattern, i.e., a de facto change in placement, then an MD must be conducted. If the behavior is an MD, then an FBA must be conducted unless the school district had conducted an FBA before the behavior that resulted in the "change of placement" occurred. They must then implement a behavioral intervention plan (a BSP for non-serious behavior; PBIP for serious behavior) for the student. If a behavioral intervention plan (BSP or PBIP) already has been developed, the team must then review the behavioral intervention plan, and modify it, as necessary, to address the behavior. See: 34 C.F.R. 300.530(f)(1).

Term	Definition	Law/ Best Practice	When Required
Function of Behavior	After analyzing the antecedents, behavior and consequences in terms of what the student gets or rejects through a behavior, the determination of the behavior's "function" is established (e.g., he runs out of the room to escape difficult seatwork; she runs out of the room to initiate a staff/student tag game). This is the first step in deciding what is supporting the problem behavior and what changes will be made to address the problem.	**Law:** This approach is mandated in federal and state law (see FBA above). **Best Practice:** All students who have not responded to typical positive school structure, appropriate curriculum and supportive relationships should receive interventions to remove behavioral barriers to academic success.	According to research in the field of applied behavior analysis, whenever a highly individualized approach to addressing a problem behavior is required, the function of the behavior must be determined in this process. Legally, this approach is <u>only</u> specifically required when a misbehavior is determined to be a manifestation of the disability. Practically, designing a behavior plan without this information is not likely to result in success. Recent "Behavioral RtI" approaches increasingly focus on school-based interventions whenever behavior is interfering with learning, regardless of whether the student has or does not have special education eligibility.
Positive Behavioral Strategies, Interventions and Supports	Non-punitive methods used by adults to alter behavior through shaping (progressive reinforcement), modeling and cueing of desired positive behaviors under specific conditions in specific locations. Whole school efforts are integrated with increasing individualization as need arises.	**Law:** IDEA/Regs require these in an IEP (e.g., BSP) when behavior has been determined to impede the learning of the student or peers. **Best Practice**: This approach should be used by all educators to support positive environments and high academic achievement.	Under IEP "consideration of special factors": If misconduct is impeding learning, the IEP team must consider these strategies. (See *www.pent.ca.gov* for positive behavioral strategies, interventions and supports as well as the BSP Desk Reference accessible on this Web site.)
Reactive Strategies	All behavior plans should focus on prevention of problems, but also must address how adults can safely manage a problem behavior if it occurs again. A reactive strategy specifies the team's best guidance on how to respond in a way that minimally disrupts the flow of instruction when correction is required.	**Law:** Ca. Ed. Code prohibits the use of specific aversives in response to problem behavior (e.g., pepper spray, seclusion, restraint not required to maintain safety). **Best Practice:** Reactive strategies should be embedded in a behavior plan that focuses on altering environments, teaching alternatives.	All behavior plans should state the four reactive strategies: 1. How to prompt the student to switch to the functionally equivalent replacement behavior; 2. How to handle the problem safely; 3. How to debrief/practice using a supportive stance; 4. School or legal consequences for infractions that may or may not be employed, depending on the severity of the misbehavior.

Term	Definition	Law/ Best Practice	When Required
Functionally Equivalent Replacement Behavior **FERB**	An acceptable, alternate behavior that allows the student to meet the same function, e.g., if the consequence is — "She escapes through loud swearing"; it might be replaced with — "She escapes through using a work 'pass' card." Ultimately we want to increase general positive behavior, such as completing all work with no complaints. However, a FERB also may be required in this process.	**Law:** Not mentioned **Best Practice:** The goal of FBA is to identify what supports problem behavior. Plans based on an FBA include both a FERB for conditional use (instead of the problem behavior) AND positive changes in the environment to support desired behaviors.	When interventions are not effective to prompt the positive desired behavior, e.g., completing work with no complaints, a FERB is allowed as an alternative. (See: www.pent.ca.gov, *Behavior Support Plan Desk Reference Manual*) A FERB is one of three components for successful behavior plans: 1. environmental supports to promote general positive behavior; 2. teaching and reinforcing FERBs that will be acceptable; and 3. specifying reactive strategies for staff use if the problem occurs again.
Behavior Support Plan **BSP** **Behavior Intervention Plan** **BIP** **Older terminology:** **Behavior Management Plan**	A behavior plan delineates what staff will do to change problem behavior. It is based on the analysis of the function of the behavior. It includes positive proactive components to support desired positive behaviors, how to teach FERBs, and what reactive strategies to use if problem behavior occurs again. It provides for on-going progress monitoring of the student's skill acquisition, decline in problem behavior and use of the FERB. For a student with an IEP, the behavior plan is a supplementary aid and support to maintain Least Restrictive Environment. LRE support is a legal requirement before more restrictive environments are considered.	**Law:** IDEA and Federal Regulations require consideration of strategies, including positive behavioral interventions when behavior impedes the learning of the student or peers. A function-based behavior plan is this consideration. (Note: In California, using the term BSP differentiates it from the more data driven, Ca. required PBIP for behaviors defined as "serious" in Ca. Ed. Code.) **Best Practice:** Use function-based behavior plans for any student whose behavior interferes with learning. If the behavior is not yet impeding learning, but may be if it continues, use other interventions, develop goals and monitor to determine if the behavior has risen to the level of interfering with learning.	**For students with IEPs:** Under the federal and state-mandated "consideration of special factors if behavior impedes learning," the IEP team is required to consider and select strategies, including positive behavioral interventions (supports) and strategies when behavior impedes learning. (This is irrespective of whether the behavior is a manifestation of disability. Selection of individual strategies in this process should be based on why the student is using the problem behavior, i.e., the function.) **RtI for behavior interventions for all students:** If general classroom positive supports, e.g., increased reinforcement, mentoring, contracts, suspensions, daily report cards, etc., to support safe, respectful and responsible behavior are ineffective, individual behavior planning based on the function of the problem behavior (BSP) is the next step. (see www.pent.ca.gov/08Law/behplansflowchart-note-mergency.pdf)

The law is clear that setting behavioral goals alone will not suffice once we have reached the "interferes-with-learning" decision. If Tier I interventions have been shown to be ineffective, the IEP team must remove this behavioral barrier to academic success. Therefore, it is imperative that Tier I interventions are solidly in place for the student with an IEP, prior to determining behavior-impedes-learning or we would be adding higher tiers of interventions on a broken base. This has been a common problem in the field.

- **RTI perspective:** The student who has not responded to Tier I, will now require Tier II positive interventions as the next step. This might include such interventions as daily report cards exchanged with the family and/or others; a check in/check out system that incorporates self-monitoring; participating in a school-based mentoring or social skills program; a behavioral contract with positive reinforcement or other positive behavioral interventions. In general, if progress monitoring indicates that these Tier II interventions are not effective, then the team must address the behavior through development of Tier III interventions, most typically a function-based plan. (See Chapter 3 for an example of Behavioral RTI-Tiers of Interventions for students with and without special education eligibility.)

If problem behaviors are an established area of need for this student, as determined by the IEP team, a behavioral goal must be developed and monitored, just as academic needs are addressed in goals that are "periodically" monitored and reported to parents. This requirement holds regardless of whether the problem has risen to the level of "impedes learning." If an IEP team is unsure as to whether this behavior has now become a behavior that impedes learning, they still must determine if this is an area of need. If this is an area of need, then a behavioral goal is required to monitor achievement of the desired general positive behavior, such as working on seatwork tasks without disrupting others. The school may continue to provide universal interventions, monitoring carefully, and as with all RTI processes, move to Tier II interventions if the goal is not met.

If the IEP team determines the student has behavior that DOES impede learning, the team must go further. They must develop positive behavioral interventions, strategies and supports to address that behavior and specify them in the IEP, in addition to the goals for progress monitoring the described interventions. If these prove ineffective, the IEP team will move to Tier III interventions, which may include functional behavioral assessment, related services such as, cognitive behavior therapy and other interventions. If these, too, prove ineffective, the IEP team continues to refine the services and will consider more restrictive placement and services within that setting when needed. Figure 4, next page, illustrates this decision process for behavior impeding learning.

Figure 4

Behavioral RTI for Students with IEPs

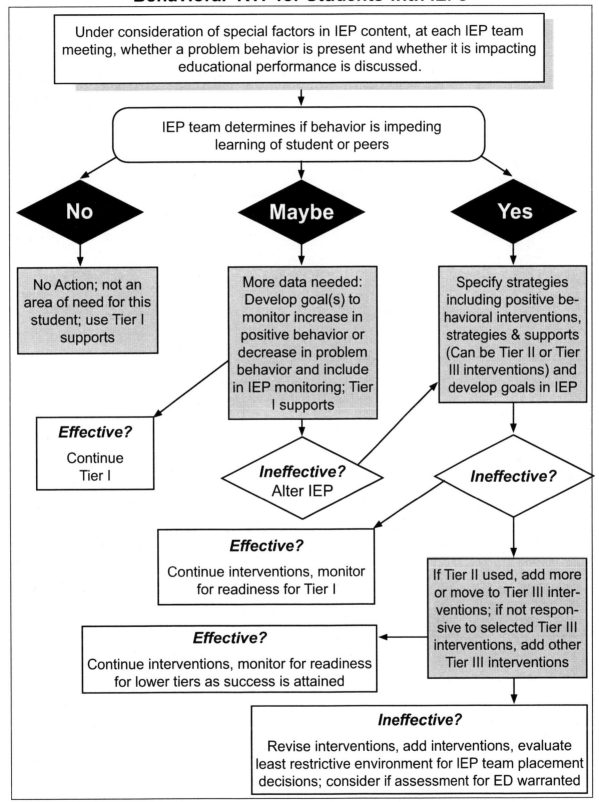

Progress Monitoring for Students with IEPs

If the student has moderate to severe intellectual disability (e.g., takes alternate state assessments), both behavioral goals and behavioral objectives or benchmarks will be required. If the student has other disabilities (e.g., takes standard state assessments with or without accommodations or modifications) only behavioral goals will be required, no benchmarks or objectives need be specifically written. In either case, however, this goal must be well written to allow progress monitoring, and the IEP team must determine the frequency of review. This must occur "periodically" according to IDEA, and reported to the parent. Some districts refer to this reporting as the "special education report card," though students with IEPs require both a standard report card and this report on goal progress. A simple one-time-a-year monitoring is not "periodic" and is not legally sufficient.

To be able to monitor progress, there must be a statement of the "baseline-level of performance" based on data in the report to the parents, which is compared to present level of performance based on data. Figure 5, next page, provides a suggested goal-writing format. The reader also is referred to *www. pent.ca.gov* for a manual on effective goal writing.

Figure 5

Formats for Writing Goals

1. To Increase General Positive Behaviors Goal

By when	Who	Will do what	At what level of proficiency	Under what conditions	Measured by whom and how
By 1/04/06,	Sam	will independently complete seatwork.	He will complete 80% of all assignments, which have been tailored to his learning needs and skills, with no prompts or reminders with 80% or better accuracy,	during science and social studies class	On 4 out of 5 days over a period of 4 consecutive weeks as recorded by teachers in their grade books.

2. Decrease Problem Behavioral Goal

By when	Who	Will do what	At what level of proficiency	Under what conditions	Measured by whom and how
By 1/04/06,	Sam's	episodes of written seatwork task refusal (loud verbal, "You can't make me!" coupled with physical withdrawal; sliding down in chair with jacket on his head)	will decrease to less than two episodes per month over a three-month period	during science and social studies classes	as measured by teacher on an Event Recording Sheet that records each event that a verbal or physical withdrawal "protest" behavior occurs.

3. Functionally Equivalent Replacement Behavior (FERB) Goal

By when	Who	Will do X behavior	For the purpose of y	Instead of Z behavior	For the purpose of y	Under what conditional conditions	At what level of proficiency	As measured by whom and how
1/07/06	Sam	will present his "pass card" to request a time away	for the purpose of escaping and protesting lengthy seatwork	instead of loud verbal work refusal and physical withdrawal	for the purpose of escaping and protesting lengthy seatwork	every time he states he needs a break, inside the math and social studies classroom	requesting it quietly without disrupting others (as taught by the teacher)	teacher recorded on event recording sheet on sheet for each episode.

Take-home Messages about RTI and Students with Disabilities

- Students with IEPs may participate in school-based RTI models for all students, but the IEP team is the monitoring team for decision-making.

- The IEP team applies the RTI logic, and determines the decision point for "behavior impeding learning" that has a requirement for specified positive behavioral interventions to be included in the IEP and monitored "periodically."

- Students with problem behaviors need goals that are periodically monitored and reported to parents; once per year will not suffice.

- Positive behaviors strategies and supports can be Tier II interventions until such time as these are shown to be ineffective and three interventions are determined to be necessary by the IEP team.

- If Tier II interventions prove ineffective, the IEP team is required to move to Tier III interventions, and finally to consideration of more restrictive settings in which interventions and services will be delivered.

When Behavior Is a Basis for Consideration of a Change in Placement

The IEP team is the authorized decision-making body in a school district determining the least restrictive environment (LRE) for a student with a disability. Legally, changes in placement due to a behavioral excess must be based on data analysis that determines academic or behavioral instruction CANNOT be delivered in the least restrictive environment. Least restrictive in legal terms, is that environment with the most access to nondisabled peers; not as some educators believe, the environment in which it would be the easiest to teach the desired curriculum or behaviors. 34 CFR 300.114, 20 USC 1412(a)(5)

- IDEA, since its inception, has been based in RTI logic. That is, data that demonstrates non-responsiveness to a lower tier of intervention is required prior to consideration of changing environments or adding interventions.

The Role of Supplementary Aids and Services in RTI

Every student with an IEP has demonstrated the need for specialized instruction and possibly related services, due to the unique nature of the identified disability. This is the definition of special education. The IEP is essentially a civil rights document, guaranteeing this student will not be discriminated against because of the disability; that is, an adequate education, a FAPE, will occur. This student, like all students, will receive a free public education, individually appropriate for the student. The IEP outlines this FAPE and identifies the least restrictive environment in which this FAPE will be delivered.

Additionally, the IDEA requires that supplementary aids and services are included in the IEP, when needed, to assist in maintaining the least restrictive environment, prior to consideration of more restrictive environments.

- **From an RTI perspective,** the level three intervention of a function-based behavior plan to address problem behavior is legally considered a supplementary aid for the purpose of maintaining least restrictive environment.

- **In support of the RTI logic,** IDEA essentially is adding protections to prevent unnecessarily restrictive environments, through the supplementary aid requirement.

Changing a placement without attempting all tiers of RTI, monitoring those interventions and reporting frequently to team members, would be a failure to provide FAPE in the LRE — the core legal requirement for students with disabilities. Yet many students have behavior plans that are not implemented, or only partially implemented, prior to consideration of placement changes.

- **Failure to apply RTI logic** related to behavior planning has resulted in findings of substantive inadequacy of the entire IEP, i.e., FAPE did not occur due to a missing behavior plan when needed, failure to monitor the plan, failure to revise unsuccessful plans, failure to train staff to implement the plan, etc. When this occurs, the typical legal outcome is attorney's fees for the prevailing party (for the parents) and compensatory education for the lost FAPE (for the student), and likely additional professional behavior analysis services to further analyze or address the behavior. These are expensive outcomes. (For an example of behavior plan errors that resulted in a lack of FAPE finding, see approximately page 63 and forward in: *www.documents.dgs.ca.gov/oah/seho_decisions/2006100159-2007031009.pdf*.)

When School Personnel Take Actions That Could Be a De Facto Change in Placement: RTI under Fire

If school administrators take actions that supersede the IEP team's authority, additional legal requirements must be met. Administration has the right to discipline all students, but the IEP team has obligations to assure those actions don't abridge FAPE.

In Relation to Suspensions (School Removals)

IDEA states that 10 days is the "FAPE-free zone." In other words, the IEP team has no voice in determining whether disciplinary removals are appropriate interventions for problem behavior for the disabled student, if those suspensions have not totaled more than 10 days in the school year. Thus, IDEA has not required any intervention occur due to disciplinary removals, if the 10 days have not been exceeded. The IDEA calls all absences from school due to the action of administration, a "removal" that must be counted toward the 10-day limit. Asking the student's family to pick up the student because "Tommy is having a bad day, let's just have you pick him up, but we won't count it as a suspension" is not in compliance with IDEA if it is not counted in the 10-day limit. Many administrators distinguish between a suspension and this type of removal, and thus do not record that action as a "disciplinary removal" subject to the 10-day rule. Thus, they easily exceed maximum removals, which can create substantial legal compliance issues and sometimes a "lack of FAPE provided" ruling can occur.

Once the 11th day has finally occurred, however, the IDEA adds two additional procedures that affect RTI logic:

Procedure One

The school personnel (typically principal or vice principal, or designee) who removes for the 11th day (and for every suspension past 10 days that occurs again) must determine that these actions do not "constitute a pattern." If, in considering the recurring nature of the behavior, the frequency of suspensions, the proximity of one suspension to the other and other factors (see *www.pent.ca.gov/forms*) that person concludes there is a pattern, then a manifestation determination IEP team meeting must occur. That means the IEP team does not need to give "permission" prior to the suspension, but that the IEP team must now meet to make crucial decisions. The school personnel may be usurping IEP team determination of placement through continued suspensions. What is FAPE for this student? This must be examined by the IEP team again. They must determine if, in relation to the problem behavior, the IEP was being implemented at the time of the problem behavior or not, and whether this disability has a direct and substantial effect on the problem behavior. If these two prongs of manifestation determination show either the IEP was not being implemented in relation to the behavior, or the disability is directly linked to the problem behavior, a functional behavioral assessment must occur (*www.pent.ca.gov*).

In RTI terms, once that 11th day of suspension is reached, RTI Tier I or Tier II interventions will not suffice, an FBA will occur, and most probably a function-based behavior plan (Tier III) will be required.

In terms of fidelity of implementation, a core RTI component, if the failure to implement a behavior plan, a component of the IEP, is related to the problem behavior occurring, no manifestation is "passed" and continuing to suspend under this condition puts the district in grave risk of a lack of FAPE finding. Teams must continually supervise the implementers of plans to maintain fidelity.

Procedure Two

The school personnel suspending the student for the 11th and every subsequent day, together with one of the student's teachers, must determine what would be necessary for the student to make progress toward IEP goals and participate in the general curriculum during the suspension (*www.pent.ca.gov/forms*). This is not the full FAPE described in detail on the IEP. Some have referred to this as a form of "FAPE light" in that not all services on the IEP are provided during the suspension.

In RTI terms, the action of the school personnel taken because of ongoing problem behavior should not result in suspension of academic tiers of intervention and support entirely during the suspension after 10 days in the school year.

In Relation to Expulsions

When the school district is considering an expulsion for a problem behavior, the primary task of the IEP team is to conduct the manifestation determination meeting. If the behavior subject to expulsion <u>was</u> determined to be a manifestation of the student's disability, due to one of either prong not having been met, no expulsion can occur and placement decisions are an IEP team function as usual. Thus, any placement change will be subject to IEP team jurisdiction for FAPE in an LRE with all supplementary aids and services to support that placement. An FBA is required, as with removals when the behavior is a manifestation. What was the student getting or rejecting with that problem behavior?

In RTI terms, a Tier III intervention will be required, i.e., a function-based behavior plan, and the IEP team will be the monitoring team. This student <u>does</u> have behavior impeding learning (i.e., s/he was nearly expelled!) and, therefore, interventions are required, not simply a return to placement, or a change in placement due to IEP decision-making on a LRE. Specifically, Level 3 is required, because interventions will most likely be based on the function of the behavior. Figures 6 and 7, next pages, provide guidance on using a three pathway function-based summary teaming procedure that links data from FBA to interventions necessary to support desired outcomes (Browning Wright, & Cook, 2008, adapted from original pathway chart from O'Neill, 1997; Sprague, 1998).

Figure 6: Part 1

Using a Three Pathway Summary Chart

What does the Three Pathway Summary Chart summarize?

All functional behavioral assessments examine the predictors for current problem behavior (immediate and immediate past antecedents to the behavior) to determine what is supporting the problem behavior as well as the maintaining consequence (function) of the behavior. This chart summarizes those findings graphically and illustrates the relationship of interventions to the FBA analysis.

What are the Three Pathways?

- **Upper Pathway:** *Intervene and alter conditions to support this path*
  General positive behavior expected of all students under similar conditions that we hope to attain through adopting the behavior plan.

- **Middle Pathway:** *Redirect to either upper or lower pathway*
  This is the problem sequence A-B-C that identifies the context of the undesirable behavior we wish to eliminate.

- **Lower Pathway:** *Teach to redirect from middle pathway*
  This is the tolerable functionally equivalent replacement behavior we wish to teach and support as an alternate to the middle pathway. When the supports put in place to gain the general positive behaviors on the upper pathway are not yet sufficient, we allow the student to achieve the same outcome as the problem behavior, only with a different form of behavior we can tolerate.

Why should I use a Pathway Chart?

Typically teams meet to address behavior problems and start discussing interventions prior to a full analysis of why the problem is occurring in the first place. This can result in behavior plans lacking clarity and breadth of analysis. When the eight steps below are followed, this chart provides a sequential problem-solving format for the team, is time-efficient and summarizes the FBA. The chart clearly communicates what is an analysis (the boxes) versus what is an intervention (the dotted arrows) and provides clarity in understanding why the behavior is occurring. It highlights the three paths that will be addressed in the behavior plan and allows the consultant to steer the team to the conceptual basis of a function-based plan. Using this approach, more consensus can be reached and interventions designed by the team can more directly address the problem.

Where do we get the data for the Pathway Summary Chart?

Complete the functional behavioral assessment data collection that included the necessary three elements of all assessments:

- Direct Observation

- Review of Records

- Interviews

129

This data will demonstrate the purpose the behavior serves for the student, and the predictors, setting events and maintaining consequences (function achieved by the behavior) that are "triggers" for the problem.

How does the team meeting use the Three Pathway Summary Chart and why?

If the lead behavior consultant collaboratively structures the team in graphing the pathways in the following order, the team will gain an understanding of the foundation of the subsequent behavior plan and opposition minimized. The necessary interventions to support success can then be addressed in the behavior plan with buy-in from all members already procured.

- **Step One:** Begin by agreeing on the problem behavior definition.

  Rationale: The team must agree on one problem behavior to graph and address in the plan. This is the logical beginning.

- **Step Two:** Agree on general positive behavior expected (what all students are expected to do). Typically the teacher will be able to easily provide this statement.

  Rationale: The teacher must readily grasp that the intent of the plan is to remove behavioral barriers to educational success. This step gains that buy in.

- **Step Three:** Agree on the outcome of the general positive behavior. Why would it be desirable for the student to use this behavior? Typically the teacher will readily provide this rationale.

  Rationale: The team has now completed the pathway that will be supported by one-third of the behavior plan through supportive interventions and environmental changes. These first three steps reassure implementers that the plan will be addressing desired outcomes as a priority.

- **Step Four:** Discuss the predictors, the triggering antecedents that are the context of the problem behavior. Your environmental analysis will have pointed out variables that support problem behavior rather than the desired positive behaviors, e.g., lengthy wait times, task complexity and skill mismatches, etc. See *www.pent.ca.gov* for environmental assessment tools in the *BSP Desk Reference*.

  Rationale: The team is now ready to look at the core problem that will need to be altered in the behavior plan.

- **Step Five:** Identify what your data analysis has yielded and your hypothesis on what is supporting the problem. What is the student getting or rejecting (avoiding, removing, protesting) by the behavior? This is the "communicative intent" of the behavior, which is the reason an FBA has been conducted.

  Rationale: The team has now identified the maintaining consequence of the behavior. The lower pathway discussed in Step Seven, below, will allow the student to meet this need through an acceptable alternative (functionally equivalent replacement behavior). We must have a consensus understanding of the purpose of the behavior before developing the functionally equivalent behavior.

- **Step Six:** Sometimes, but not always, immediate past antecedents or setting events strengthen the likelihood that on this day, at this time, in this situation, the student is especially likely to use problem behavior when confronted by the triggering antecedents. The teacher and family may have data to contribute in this section. The behavior plan will address altering the environment, task or instruction when the setting event occurs in order to reduce the likelihood of problem behavior.

    Rationale: The team will wish to pre-plan how to prevent escalation if setting events, periodic variables, strengthen the possibility that environmental variables will trigger problem behavior. If the team brings up constantly occurring variables, such as parent neglect, presence of a disability, etc., the consultant can demonstrate that this is "off the chart" and dealt with through other interventions, such as counseling, agency referrals, etc.

- **Step Seven:** This is the most difficult element of function-based behavior analysis for most teams. The consultant will need to point out that for some students, this is only a temporary step until such changes to support the upper pathway are systematically addressed. For other more complex cases, this lower pathway will be needed continuously. For example, if the student runs out of the room because he wished to escape difficult work, our primary upper pathway interventions will be designed to increase task compliance through altering work or providing supports to aid completion.

    Rationale: There likely will be times when the student begins the tried and true middle pathway, e.g., terminate a task by running away. Rather, we want this function to be achieved with a different behavior form, such as putting work in a "break now" folder. The task is terminated through the lower pathway method and the middle path is eliminated. Once we have charted this final lower pathway, and the team has reached consensus, the behavior plan can be more rapidly and skillfully completed.

Note: This pathway chart was revised by Diana Browning Wright and Clayton R. Cook and is based on an original Three Pathway Summary Chart developed by O'Neill, R. E., Horner, R. H., Albin, R. W., Sprague, J. R., Newton, S., and Storey, K. (1997). Functional assessment and program development for problem behavior: A practical handbook (2nd ed.). *Pacific Grove, CA: Brookes/Cole.*

Figure 6: Part 2

Consultant's Script for Pathway Charting

Opening: *Let's begin by graphically illustrating why we think this problem is occurring, and once we have a working hypothesis diagrammed, we will move on to designing interventions to address the problem.* (Place Pathway diagram on chart paper, overhead, or projected computer screen to focus team on the analysis, not the consultant.) *Those interventions will be in three areas: what we can do to help this* *student perform well in school — the upper pathway; how we can prevent and safely handle the problem if it occurs again — the middle pathway; and, then, how we can develop an acceptable alternative when our efforts to achieve the upper pathway are not entirely effective — the lower pathway. Our behavior plan will be built on this three pathway analysis we are about to begin. The science of behavior is built on core beliefs that behavior is learned, and that lasting change occurs when we approach behavior change from a positive behavioral intervention perceptive. Thus, our plan will be built on developing student skills, reinforcing desired behavior, and altering environments to remove variables that lead to problem behavior or adding variables that would support the desired behaviors. This pathway process will help us focus our thinking of how we can accomplish this.*

Point to each box on your blank Three Pathway Summary as you complete this sequence.

First Step: *Let's describe the behavior in such a way that anyone would know what we are talking about. So, we can't just say he/she is defiant; we need to describe what it looks and sounds like when a behavior we call defiant is occurring. How shall we describe this problem behavior?*

Second Step: *What exactly would we want this student to be doing at the time the problem occurs? What are all the students doing that we consider positive behavior, for example, are the students working on tasks we have assigned? This is the general positive behavior that supports academic and social success.* (Turn to the teacher(s) present for your lead on steps two and three.)

Third Step: *If the student is engaged in the second step general positive behaviors, what would be the typical consequence or educational outcome for the students?*

Fourth Step: *Ok, exactly what are the variables present, the antecedents, to this problem behavior? Looking at the environmental analysis we conducted, let's discuss these observations.* Review your observations of what is present that you hypothesize is the trigger for the problem behavior. Remember to use "not yet" if a variable is not present that therefore results in the student engaging in the problem, e.g., "Johnny has not yet been taught an individual schedule to anticipate what is coming next in his day."

Fifth Step: *Let's consider this now from the student's perspective. Something happens after this behavior that supports the student choosing this behavior. It has worked in the past and is working now to produce something the student desires. The science of behavior analysis says all behavior is learned, and that behavior is reinforced, and occurs again and again because of an outcome. That outcome is either (1) getting something or (2) rejecting something (avoiding, protesting or escaping something). Let's examine our data and experience with this student and generate a hypothesis that summarizes this chain of events.*

Sixth Step: *Ok, I think we now have a pretty clear picture of what we want the student to be doing, and a pretty clear picture of the triggers for our problem. Now, has anyone noticed any periodically occurring events that make it even more likely that when confronted by the antecedents we have identified that XXX will use the problem behavior? For example, when he doesn't sit in the usual spot, when someone has said something unpleasant to him, when he is late for school, etc. We call these "setting events," and we want to be sure to have an intervention to use in our plan if a setting event is present.*

Seventh Step: *Now we come to the hardest part of a function-based analysis. We are going to design a plan that helps XXX do the desired alternative positive behavior. And, our plan will block XXX from using the problem behavior to get or reject what we have identified. But to achieve that, we will want to consider acceptable alternative behavior that allows him to either get or reject, but through using a* *different behavior. The function will be the same, but the form of the behavior will be different. For some students this will be a tolerable, temporary behavior, and we can expect that it will be chosen less and less by the student as the supports we put in place for the upper pathway become more effective. For other students with greater behavioral challenges, and often greater general skill deficits or intellectual disability, we may wish to encourage this behavior for a longer period of time.*

Summarize: *So, we have outlined three distinct pathways.* (Point and describe the graphed content you have just charted.) *The upper pathway we will support through interventions, environmental changes and increasing reinforcement for the desired behavior.* (Gesture the upper pathway.) *The middle pathway we will block through ways we prompt replacement behaviors, and how we react to the problem if it occurs.* (Gesture the middle pathway.) *The lower pathway is the tolerable path we will teach, reinforce and prompt the student to use.* (Gesture the lower pathway.)

Moving Functional Assessment to Behavior Planning: *We are now ready to design the interventions that match the analysis we have just completed. Our plan will include environmental changes that support XXX in achieving the desired positive behaviors we want.* (Gesture the upper pathway and read the content of the dotted arrows.) *Our plan will specify how to prompt the student to use either the upper pathway or the lower pathway when triggering antecedents are present.* (Gesture the dotted arrows between triggering antecedents and problem behavior.) *Our plan will describe how staff should respond after the problem behavior is present, either allowing the student to switch to the acceptable alternative or the desired alternative.* (Gesture the two reactive strategies up and down.)

We also will describe how to handle the problem safely if our intervention did not divert the behavior, (gesture to arrow between problem behavior and maintaining consequence) *and how we will debrief with the student or apply school based consequences if required following the students return to acceptable behavior.* (Gesture to the straight arrow reactive strategies to the right of the maintaining consequences box.)

Preview the Behavior Plan Sequence: *We are now ready to develop a function-based behavior support plan based on our analysis. As we complete this process, let's keep referring to our analysis we just charted to be sure our interventions directly address the problem. Here is a preview of how other teams have found they can address this process efficiently:*

- *Let's begin by addressing the environmental changes we need to put in place and how we can reinforce this student more effectively for either pathway.* (Gesture to the line 7 arrows-environmental changes, and line 11-reinforcement.)

- *After we finish the upper pathway interventions, we will be ready to address the lower pathway, functional equivalent behavior, how we will teach, reinforce and prompt this behavior and going back and adding any environmental changes we will need to facilitate this pathway, line 9.*

- *Finally, we will address the middle pathway, the reactive strategies we will use to prevent the expression of the problem behavior, line 12, section 1, 2, 3, 4.*

Figure 7

Three-Pathway Function-Based Summary: FBA and Intervention Planning

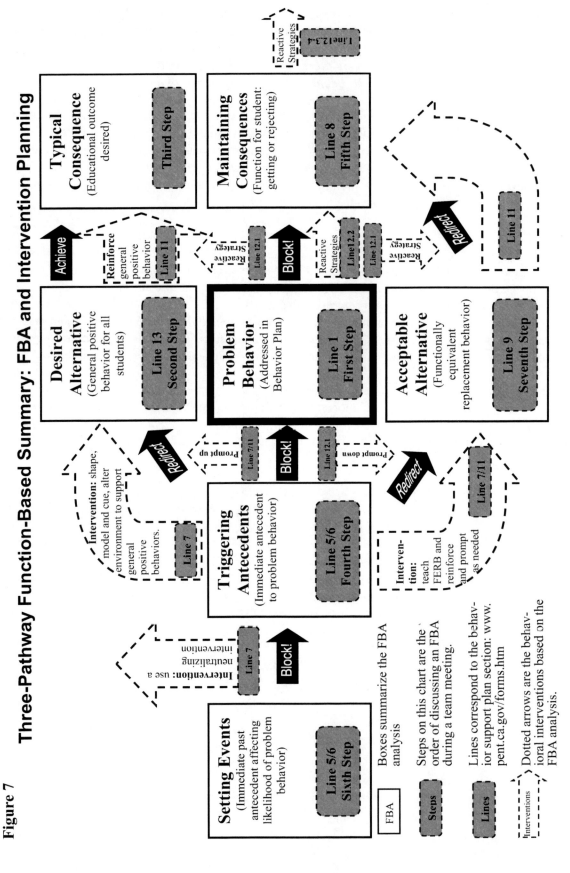

Browning Wright & Cook, 2008: See *BSP Desk Reference* for plan development instructions: *www.pent.ca.gov.*

Student's Behavior <u>Was Not</u> Manifestation of the Disability

No FBA is required if student's behavior, subject to expulsion, was not a manifestation of his disability, although most districts will choose to perform one to aid in behavior plan development. The student will still be entitled to FAPE during the expulsion period, and obviously there is a behavioral need that must be addressed to assure the behavior does not reoccur in whatever placement the student will be in during the expulsion, even if that placement is home teaching.

- **In RTI terms**, the student will receive a Tier III intervention due to the severity of the problem that resulted in an expulsion. All students with IEPs must receive an education during the expulsion.

45-School Day Removals for Weapons, Drugs and Extremely Dangerous Behavior

School personnel may remove the student for weapons, drugs and extremely dangerous behavior to a 45-school day placement while all disciplinary procedures are completed. This provision is to allow the school the time necessary to complete all expulsion and resolution of differences proceedings. These 45 days allow sufficient time to determine the next course of action without the risk of the student returning to campus before these critical decisions are reached. During this 45-day placement, the IEP team determines if the placement is sufficient for the student, and must determine "services to be sure the behavior does not reoccur."

- **In RTI terms**, the student will receive behavior support beyond Tier I. The IEP team will consider the necessary tier of intervention, and will most likely conclude that Tier III supports, such as a function-based behavior plan and/or additional related services are required.

Role of Related Services for Students with IEPs

Students with IEPs require consideration of whether related services to benefit from their special education are needed. In relation to behavior, these services frequently equate to mental health service provider services, such as cognitive behavior therapy or family therapy and, on some occasions, medical evaluation (for diagnostic purposes only). 34 CFR 300.34

- **In RTI logic**, to determine if these services are required, an adverse effect on special education provided services must be shown. Since related services are well beyond Tier I and Tier II interventions, as well as more intensive than a function-based behavior plan, the team most often will wish to implement a function-based plan prior to determining related services are required.

Role of RTI for Students Whose Status Is Changed to Emotionally Disturbed

When a student's behavior has not responded to the tiers of intervention, often IEP teams question whether the disabling condition has been correctly identified. Typically, the assessment plan will be to determine whether the student has an emotional disturbance because of failure to respond to lesser interventions, and, therefore, further assessment and consideration of an emotional disturbance label is warranted.

Although all students with IEPs are entitled to any service determined as necessary by the IEP team once eligibility for any of the 13 disabilities is established, some districts believe only certain services are available, depending on the disability. For example, the erroneous belief that the related services of mental health must be "qualified" for by the determination of emotional disturbance or a specific placement "qualified for" by eligibility as emotionally disturbed. There is only one qualification in special education, and that is qualification for special education services. Every service added, or placement considered, is up to the IEP team to determine without any "qualifying" for that service or placement.

- **RTI implication:** When a student with an IEP has not responded to behavioral interventions available for all students, the IEP team will wish to consider related services whether or not the student has an emotionally disturbed label. Related services are typically considered Tier III interventions from an RTI perspective. If the student does not respond to these either the team will likely conclude there are grounds for a more restrictive placement, and perhaps further assessment to determine if "Emotional Disturbance" is a disability for this student.

Role of RTI for Students Already Assessed as Emotionally Disturbed and Eligible for Special Education

The eligibility for special education under the criteria of "emotional disturbance" is education based (i.e., depends on the student's observable behavioral and emotional responses in school). If the student does not demonstrate observable problem responses in school, any emotional disturbance that is or was identified by outside providers, would not be sufficient grounds for special education eligibility. Eligibility, then, typically will cease when tiers of interventions succeed. The IDEA requires that the IEP team and other qualified professionals review existing evaluation data on the child, including evaluations provided by the parents; current classroom-based, local or state assessments, and classroom-based observations; and observations by teachers and related services providers. 34 CFR 300.305. This response to interventions analysis considers all available data in this determination.

- **RTI implication:** When the student increasingly responds to behavioral RTI, then the student is essentially on the way to eliminating the educational diagnosis of emotional disturbance. Tiers of interventions occur in all settings, in general education and in restrictive placements.

What Schools Must Remember about RTI for Students with Disabilities

In conclusion, schools must remember the unique RTI requirements for a student with an IEP. The IEP team, which must consist of parents, an administrator, general education teacher and special education staff, must systematically address any behavior problems that are preventing educational progress, just as they are required to address academic barriers to success. As was described, when behavior impedes learning, addressing this behavior must include positive interventions. If the behavior was so serious that excessive disciplinary removals (suspensions) or recommendations for involuntary placement changes or expulsions occur, a manifestation determination analysis must be conducted. Legally the requirement is for a Tier III intervention (Functional Behavioral Assessment) if that analysis shows the behavior was a direct result of a disability or resulted from a failure to implement a portion of the IEP related to the behavior.

Additionally, if the student is removed for 45 school days, services must be specified in the IEP to be sure the behavior does not reoccur in that setting, which again points to the likely provision of Tier III supports.

As can be determined by reviewing this chapter, the school must make sure function-based behavior plans are written with skill. Methods for training school staff to develop legally valid and educationally impactful behavior support plans have been studied. Research has shown that training on the key concepts alone is not sufficient to improve educators' skills and knowledge to develop high-quality, behavior supports plans. Rather, training that operationalizes the key concepts and provides trainees with the opportunity to practice writing plans and receive feedback based on their performance is a more effective approach to training, which improves educators' competency at developing workable behavior support plans (Browning Wright, Mayer, Cook, Crews, Kraemer, & Gale, 2007; Kraemer, Cook, Browning Wright, Mayer, & Wallace, in press).

To put the importance of training in context, a recent study has shown that the evidence-based quality of behavior support plans (i.e., extent to which plans are written to include critical research-based content) is related positively and strongly to reductions in problem behaviors, increases in functionally equivalent replacement behavior(s), increases in general positive behaviors, and improvements in academic performance (Cook, 2008).

References

Browning Wright, D., & Cook, C.R. (2008). Methods of developing a three pathway function based summary. Retrieved April 12, 2008, from *www.pent.ca.gov*.

Browning Wright, D., Mayer, G. R., Cook, C. R., Crews, D., Kraemer, B. R., & Gale, B. (2007). A preliminary study on the effects of training using behavior support plan quality evaluation guide (BSP-QE) to improve positive behavioral support plans. *Education and Treatment of Children, 30,* 89-106.

Cook, C. R., Crews, D., Wright, D. B., Mayer, R., Gale, B., & Kraemer, B. (2007). Establishing and evaluating the substantive adequacy of positive behavior support plans. *Journal of Behavioral Education, 16,* 191-206.

Cook, C. R. (2008). *Exploring the link between evidence-based positive behavior support plans and student outcomes: An initial effectiveness study.* (Doctoral dissertation, University of California, Riverside. Dissertation Abstracts International.)

Kraemer, B. R., Cook, C. R., Browning Wright, D., Mayer, G. R., & Wallace, M. D. (in press). Effects of training on the use of the behavior support plan quality evaluation guide with autism educators: a preliminary investigation examining positive behavior support plans. *Journal of Positive Behavioral Interventions.*

O'Neill, R. E., Horner, R. H., Albin, R. W., Sprague, J. R., Newton, S., & Storey, K. (1997). *Functional assessment and program development for problem behavior: A practical handbook* (2nd ed.). Pacific Grove, CA: Brookes/Cole.

Sprague, J. R., Sugai, G., & Walker, H. (1998). Antisocial behavior in schools. In T. S. W. F. M. Gresham (Ed.), *Handbook of child behavior therapy* (pp. 451-474). New York: Plenum.

Chapter Seven

Pre-Planning to Avoid Staff Resistance to Adopting and Implementing Behavioral RTI

After reading this chapter, you will be able to:

➤ summarize what this book has provided;

➤ describe the Belief System Barrier to Achievement;

➤ administer a staff survey instrument to assess potential staff resistance due to erroneous belief systems;

➤ identify knowledge barriers and content required for effective implementation at the classroom and school levels;

➤ summarize skills needed for effective implementation; and

➤ identify exemplary procedures at district- and school-site level that lead to successful adoption, implementation, and maintenance of evidence-based practices.

What It Takes to Succeed at Change

Throughout the country, schools have responded to No Child Left Behind mandates by seeking higher achievement scores, and they are more receptive than ever before to changing how they operate. Despite this apparent receptivity, the authors have encountered districts and schools whose interest has waned after an initial, enthusiastic endorsement with intentions to adopt new practices. "Business as usual" returns, with the same low outcomes as before. What went wrong? Can we analyze barriers, pre-plan to achieve desired results and avoid this? What are the causes of the backsliding and lack of success some systems encounter?

As we know, schools all over the country, such as those described in Chapter 5, have succeeded. Failing schools often state their students' characteristics are the primary, substantial reason for the school or individual teacher's lack of success in achieving better outcomes. Yet, across the country, highly successful schools with challenging characteristics of ethnic diversity, poverty, parental disengagement, and English language learners have substantially improved achievement through more effective interventions in academic and schoolwide behavior through positive supports and behavioral RTI structures (McIntosh, Chard, Boland, & Horner, 2006; Sadler, 2000).

As discussed throughout this book, the successful district and school site must mobilize resources to:

- develop viable systems that identify students in need of the correct level of behavioral supports;

- convince staff that removing behavioral barriers to educational success is our responsibility and the students' right;

- effectively integrate behavioral RTI with academic RTI efforts;

- support and enforce fidelity of interventions until data-based decisions to change the intervention has occurred;

- create strong leadership commitment and an enthusiastic and collaborative team willing and able to systematically apply evidence-based interventions with skill;

- protect time and place for regularly occurring team meeting to analyze individual and whole school data on improved outcomes; and

- provide coaching, training, and staff reinforcement on interactions and environmental changes that support general positive behaviors.

So what prevents schools and districts from taking these important steps? We believe that barriers to success can be categorized in four areas: Beliefs, Knowledge, Skills, and Procedures. Each category can be analyzed for barriers, and preplanning can occur to avoid the pitfalls that result in stagnation or failure. Leaders in school reform efforts and schoolwide positive behavior supports initiatives have often stated that 80 percent of the staff must want to change and support the efforts if training is to be effective and we are to achieve the desired outcomes. Without this endorsement, change efforts are plagued with noncompliance and limited commitment (Sprague & Golly, 2004; Sprague & Walker, 2005).

The primary barrier to success is the will to change. Altering beliefs is best achieved through reinforcing staff who have demonstrated positive beliefs, coaching those that vacillate, providing models of peers who are successful with desirable foundational beliefs, and finally assisting those that remain stubbornly resistant to necessary core values in seeking alternative employment. The school must consider altering six core belief clusters. Behavioral RTI change agents, administrators and leaders may wish to assess the foundational beliefs that may support or hinder change efforts. An assessment process for this includes: (1) assessing Beliefs that Support Success with Behavioral RTI (Figure 1), (2) Core Beliefs that Support Improving Behavior in Schools (Figure 2), (3) Record Sheet for Beliefs about Behavior (Figure 3), (4) Data Analysis of Core Beliefs that Support Behavioral RTI (Figure 4), and (5)Behavioral RTI Receptivity Analysis (Figure 5). (All are included at the end of this chapter.)

Belief System Barriers

We can be empowered or disabled by our beliefs. The following six clusters can both support success or impede school performance, depending on what values we support.

- **Purpose of schools and teaching:** Are schools only responsible for academic skill acquisition? Or, are schools more broadly accountable for social emotional competence?

- **Relationship of environment and instruction to behavior problems:** Are we accountable for addressing the quality of programming and instruction, the Tier I host environment?

- **What the student is entitled to receive in a classroom:** Should students receive individualized supports, or are differentiated instruction and behavior supports appropriate?

- **How behaviors of students are best changed:** Should teams develop and monitor plans for fidelity? Should positive supports be used over punitive?

- **Responsibility for change:** Is it the *school's, teacher's, parent's*, or *student's* responsibility to change?

- **The importance of collaborative "communities of practice" or "professional learning communities" in supporting behavioral change, in addition to Behavioral RTI teams:** How committed are staff to the improvement of the whole school?

Knowledge Barriers

We often respond to a need for change by training staff on what is necessary to alter behavior. Yet, when the underlying belief system has not been altered, the new knowledge is not embraced, and business as usual returns until the "new, new thing" comes along and training on that is provided. Frequently, the "new" training has the same essential core underpinnings, yet with differences in terminology that initially convinced staff this is "new" and perhaps more palatable, requiring less efforts. This cycle has plagued school reform in all areas.

Core knowledge areas for Behavioral RTI include:

- **How to support schools and classrooms in providing solid Tier I structure.** Without foundational educational excellence, too many customers will need higher levels of intervention. Support must be offered on a strong base to know whether the student has the need, or the host environment is defective.

- **How to deliver group and general default positive systems for Tier II successes.** Simple check in/check out, daily home-school notes, self-management techniques and mentoring have been shown to be effective Tier II interventions (Crone & Horner, 2003).

- **How to conduct Functional Behavioral Assessments and design corresponding function-based behavior plans for Tier III successes.** Without training, the analysis will be flawed, and, therefore, the corresponding highly individualized behavior supports ineffective. (See Chapter 6, Figure 6 for a Three Pathway Analysis Procedure.)

- **How to reach the most complex students with needs for cognitive behavioral therapy and highly individualized mental health, family treatment and multi-agency involvement for Tier III successes.** Without an understanding of how to integrate these services, and which students might require which interventions, success will not be attained for the more deeply troubled students.

- **How to structure team meetings; reinforce participation and commitment in implementing behavioral supports.** Without solid procedural structures in place, time-efficient and effective data management and intervention design will fail.

- **How to achieve top-down supports, from superintendent to district administrators to school boards in committing to integrated Academic and Behavioral RTI.** Without this mandate, site implementation can stagnate.

Skill Barriers

Training that is not supported by ongoing coaching, teaming, and peer collaboration opportunities frequently results in no implementation, partial, or inaccurate implementation. When the objectives are then not met, schools blame the intervention rather than examining the problem with fidelity that is endemic in schools who fail in implementing integrated academic and behavioral RTI. It is important that the skills discussed in training sessions and team meetings are reinforced, prompted, coached, and supported through structures adopted by the school team.

Skills include staff members' ability to:

- establish situation-specific rules and well-organized procedures in every classroom and in all campus locations;

- teach positive behaviors to achieve desired consequences;

- shape (reinforce closer and closer approximations to desired behavior), model, and prompt desired general positive behaviors from staff and students;

- analyze behavior to determine triggering antecedents and maintaining consequences;

- understand and be able to design a "goodness of fit" required for students with high-support needs. This need is due to specific student characteristics, including those with disabilities impacting their behavior; and

- implement schoolwide behavior supports and reinforcement for staff and students.

Procedural Barriers

Even with the best of intentions, and even with supportive belief systems, if the school continues with procedures that support a different belief system, behavioral RTI gradually becomes subverted to the old beliefs. For example, if the procedures necessary for decision-making and progress monitoring activities are not adopted, supported, and prioritized, the team can return to previous practices (e.g., that the purpose of any school team is to either assess for special education and a new placement, or for students with eligibility already established, to press for a move to more restrictive placement).

Exemplary district-level procedural supports include:

- Requiring data reporting and aggregating across sites of student achievement <u>correlated</u> with academic and behavioral interventions that were provided for those not "meeting" or "exceeding" academic standards and/or behavioral expectations and the students' response to intervention.

- Examining office discipline referrals in all schools, and correlating that with each of those students' academic profiles and with all interventions and tiers of support provided to them in both academics and behavior.

- Providing reinforcement from school boards and district-level administrators in terms of accolades, awards, praise, and public acknowledgements for site and individual achievement. This is delivered to site administrators and staff for their achievements in the sites' increasing supports for needy students, as well as overall site academic achievement.

Exemplary site procedural supports include:

- Providing allocated and protected time for RTI problem-solving teams.

- Providing praise and other reinforcement for staff members who adopt and implement behavioral (and academic) supports for an individual student as a result of working with the problem-solving team. This should be copiously delivered to the staff member by individuals who are most valued by each implementer.

- Using methods of data collection and aggregation of data by implementers or staff who support classroom are supervised and reinforced through the problem-solving team process

Other Issues

It is important for behavioral RTI teams to write interventions with enough specificity and skill for implementers to be able to apply those interventions with skill. Periodically, the team should evaluate the clarity of their writing, seeking information from implementers on how they can improve. Progress-monitoring methods, once identified, must be monitored at the agreed-upon times, with no exceptions or fidelity is likely to be compromised.

Summary

Throughout this book we have tried to give both information gleaned from research and personal insights from our collective experience guiding districts and sites in establishing and maintaining effective academic and behavioral RTI integrated systems. We strongly encourage school teams attempting to establish or maintain RTI systems to thoughtfully examine this material.

Figure 1

Beliefs That Support Success with Behavioral RTI

Belief Area	Supportive	Non-Supportive
Purpose of schools and teaching	All schools and all staff are responsible for teaching both academics and behavior; schools are preparing students for postsecondary school and work as well as how to be a positive member of society.	Schools are responsible for academics; parents and the students themselves are responsible for their behaviors; what happens after K-12 is not the responsibility of schools.
Relationship of environment and instruction to behavior problems	How students perform is directly related to environmental structure, instructional strategies, curriculum/task and behavior support provided to meet the standards. We need to examine the "match" for the students, the Tier I provisions for academics and behavior, and change environmental variables as needed. 80-90% of all students will respond and succeed in this environment with no additional interventions; even students with disabilities.	Students must learn to "get along" and "do their work," following the established procedures and teaching methods in each environment. If a student is not succeeding, lack of motivation or laziness is the problem. Other classes should be considered as the next step.
What the student is entitled to receive in a classroom	All students are entitled to unconditional positive interactions from staff, regardless of their behaviors or achievement. All students are entitled to differentiated instruction and behavioral supports to facilitate success. If an intervention does not work, we should try new ones until success is met.	If students behave and succeed, they are entitled to teacher praise. Teachers cannot be expected to individualize academics and behavior support! If we try an intervention and it does not work, that is the student's problem. Students should behave and learn. That is their responsibility, not mine.

continues

continued

Belief Area	Supportive	Non-Supportive
How behaviors of students are best changed	Through team-based problem-solving and progress monitoring, the identified supports are developed and monitored. Doing all the interventions as written is important for decision-making on tiers needed. Positive behavioral interventions, strategies, and supports produce lasting behavioral change. Quick fix aversive interactions or punishment does not produce the best outcomes, with lasting change.	If the student has a problem, we should attempt punishment before trying other options. Teachers, combined with disciplinarians, should hold the student accountable. Teams are not necessary. Students must respect staff before staff can show them respect.
Responsibility for change lies with whom? The district or school site administration? Teachers? Parents? Students?	It is through the combined efforts of all, district and school administration, teachers, parents and students, working hand in hand that we achieve lasting change and address the unique behavior support needs of each individual student so that "No child is left behind" either because of academic or behavioral deficits. All students are entitled to our best problem-solving efforts before alternative sites or more restrictive placements are considered.	We should not have to change our current practices to collectively problem solve each student's needs. All students should adhere to our district and site policies. If they cannot, or will not comply, then we should be providing other sites for those students as quickly as possible, such as expanding "opportunity" or "alternate schools" for those that do not fit in.
The importance of collaborative "communities of practice" or "professional learning communities" as well as an RTI team in supporting behavioral change	When teams work together, using a defined protocol that is time-efficient, to analyze teaching pedagogy, curriculum content, and classroom procedures and structures, everyone can learn from everyone else. This provides inspiration for working smarter, not harder, and achieving higher outcomes. Achieving standards is not about teaching faster or raising our expectations, it is about teaching more skillfully. Working alone in classrooms by ourselves does not provide the incentives for excellence that collaborative efforts provide. This is true in addressing behavioral and academic challenges.	Having all these "meetings" about a student's behavior or academics just interferes with teachers preparing their lessons, and does nothing for addressing the day-to-day challenges of teaching to the standards. If everyone would just leave teachers alone, they could have more time to design better lessons. Team meetings never run smoothly and stick to the topics at hand, and there is just no way to correct that.

Source: Diana Browning Wright.

Figure 2

Survey on Core Beliefs about Behavior in Schools

The following beliefs are present in our schools. Please honestly evaluate your own beliefs about each statement. Record your evaluation on the accompanying record sheet (Figure 3):
1=strongly disagree   2=somewhat disagree   3=undecided   4=somewhat agree
5=strongly agree

1. Having more meetings, either about students' behavior or academics interferes with my lesson preparation and does nothing to address the daily challenges of teaching to the standards. Communication is not essential in building a knowledgeable, responsible, respectful community. Teamwork is not the key to overall school improvement

2. Schools are responsible for <u>teaching</u> both academics and behavior; schools are preparing students for postsecondary school and work as well as how to be a positive member of society, and addressing behavior is part of that work.

3. My students must respect me before I can show respect to them.

4. If everyone would just leave teachers alone, they could have more time to design better lessons, and students' behavior would improve.

5. Students must learn to "get along" and to "do their work" following my procedures and with my established teaching methods. If the student is not succeeding, lack of motivation or laziness is the problem, maybe he or she should be enrolled in other classes.

6. The reform movements have gotten carried away; I should just be allowed to teach and deal with behavior the way I always have — I'm a professional!

7. How students perform behaviorally is directly related to environmental structure. I provide, my instructional strategies and the tasks I design to meet the standards.

8. If students cannot or will not behave, we should provide other sites for those students as quickly as possible, such as expanding our "opportunity" or "alternate schools" for those that don't fit in.

9. If a student has a behavior problem, I try punishment first before exploring other options.

10. I support a team working together using defined steps that are time-efficient to analyze my classroom environment, and teaching methods and classroom procedures to improve the match for a student in my classroom having behavior problems. Working by myself in a classroom does not give me enough incentive to change what I do.

11. If students behave and succeed, they are entitled to my praise. I cannot be expected to individualize academics and behavioral supports.

12. At our school, if I use effective behavior support strategies, I can get 80%-90% of my students to achieve grade-level behavioral expectations; the other 20% will likely need my careful attention to meet those behavioral expectations.

13. If a behavior intervention does not work, I believe I should try new ones until success is met.

14. Schools are responsible for academics; parents and the students themselves are responsible for their behaviors.

15. I believe it is my responsibility to specifically teach the behaviors I want, then continuously review and reward adherence throughout the year

16. What happens after K-12 is not the responsibility of schools.

17. In my class, I am fair, and all students get the same response from me, because that is what "fairness" is all about.

18. It is through the combined efforts of all, district and school administration, teachers, parents and students, working hand in hand, that we achieve lasting change and address the unique behavior support needs of each student.

19. When a team meets to identify behavior supports, I believe doing all the interventions, exactly as described is important.

20. All students are entitled to differentiated instruction and behavioral supports to facilitate success.

21. Teaching standards is not about teaching faster or raising expectations, it is about teaching more skillfully.

22. Students should behave and study to learn the material. This is their responsibility, not mine.

23. All students are not entitled to our best problem-solving efforts before alternative sites or more restrictive placements are considered.

24. All my students are entitled to my unconditional positive interactions, regardless of their behavior or achievement.

25. Positive behavioral interventions, strategies and supports produce lasting behavioral change; quick fix aversive interventions or punishment does not produce the best results.

26. Only students with IEPs are entitled to differentiation of instruction or behavior support.

27. Our school should not allow students with emotional disabilities to be in general education classes; they always learn and behave best in separate classrooms.

28. If I do some of the interventions from a team's suggestion, I believe I am doing a good job of attempting to change the behavior.

29. It is my responsibility to help my students learn to behave.

30. The primary reason students misbehave in school is their lack of parent support.

Figure 3

Record Sheet for Beliefs about Behavior

1	
2	
3	
4	
5	
6	
7	
8	
9	
10	
11	
12	
13	
14	
15	
16	
17	
18	
19	
20	
21	
22	
23	
24	
25	
26	
27	
28	
29	
30	

Figure 4

Data Analysis

A Review of the Survey on Core Beliefs about Behavior

Although some belief statements on the survey could be considered relevant in multiple areas, the following six clusters should be analyzed to determine the extent to which supportive belief systems are present at a school site for successful reform efforts in the area of behavior.

- Purpose of schools and teaching

- Relationship of environment/instruction to behavior problems

- What the student is entitled to receive in a classroom

- How behaviors of students are best changed

- Responsibility for change rests with whom

- Importance of Community of Practice (CoP) or Professional Learning Communities (PLC) and an RTI team in supporting behavioral change

When 80% of school and district staff have supportive belief systems, real, substantive achievement can occur! Examine your own, and your schools' beliefs in the six areas most likely to affect adoption, maintenance and success of behavioral RTI efforts. Staff support of these efforts will likely fall into the following five percentage groups over time. By examining belief system at the outset, staff is encouraged to rethink underlying assumptions. Reform change agents (e.g., administrators, team leaders) will want to have a clear understanding of the belief challenges present at the school site prior to beginning change efforts. Periodic reassessment also may be fruitful.

- **20% early, enthusiastic adopters of supportive beliefs** — usually intrinsic motivated. Most likely already have supportive beliefs or will adopt rapidly.

- **20% second wave adopters** — influenced by observing top 20% role models and reinforcement from site leadership.

- **20% middle of the road** — influenced by procedures set in place and peer collaboration opportunities with the top 40% and reinforcement for change from leadership.

- **20% late wave** — influenced by specific, individual feedback on their performance from administrators as well as peer coaching on practices in alignment with supportive beliefs from the top 60%.

- **20% very late or never adopters** — despite peer supports, coaching and administrative guidance, and these entrenched staff may need to examine why their belief systems are not changing, and whether other job sites or occupations might better meet their needs. As one Arizona principal succinctly told his staff, "You are either on the bus, or in the exhaust."

Your staff anonymously completed the survey and turn in results. Do this at all staff meetings to get 100% turn-in rates. Tabulate responses. Prepare to address these belief barriers in staff development activities.

Pose questions: What percentage of our staff agreed with non-supportive beliefs? What percentage agreed with supportive beliefs? Return the blank questionnaire to staff. Have them examine the Answer Key and discuss your site's percentages in each area, item by item.

> **For Example:** "On item one, a non-supportive belief system, 30% of us disagreed with the statement and 70% of us agreed. That means 70% of us are holding erroneous beliefs about behavior and our role in addressing it. Where will we get the motivation and commitment to establish and maintain Behavioral RTI without altering our beliefs? What are the barriers? Let's discuss this now in small groups."

Figure 5

Behavioral RTI Receptivity Analysis

Cluster	Supportive Items	Non-Supportive Items
Cluster 1 purpose of education	**2, 29** *8-10=RTI supportive* *6-7= coaching need* *2-5=non-supportive, an area of concern*	**16, 30,14** *12-15= non-supportive, an area of concern; 10-11= coaching need* ***3-9=supportive***
Cluster 2 relation of environment, instruction, behavior	**7, 12** ***8-10=RTI supportive*** *6-7= coaching need* *2-5=non-supportive, an area of concern*	**5, 26, 27** *12-15= non-supportive, an area of concern; 10-11= coaching need* ***3-9=RTI supportive***
Cluster 3 student entitlement	**13, 20, 24** *12-15=RTI supportive* *7-11=coaching needed* *3-6=non-supportive, an area of concern*	**11, 22** *8-10=non-supportive area of concern* *5-7= coaching needed* ***2-4=RTI supportive***
Cluster 4 behavior change	**19, 25** ***8-10= RTI supportive*** *6-7= coaching need* *2-5=non-supportive, an area of concern*	**3, 9, 17, 28** *16-20=non-supportive area of concern* *9-15=coaching needed* ***4-8=RTI supportive***
Cluster 5 responsibility for change	**15, 18** ***8-10=RTI supportive*** *6-7= coaching need* *2-5=non-supportive, an area of concern*	**8, 23** *8-10=non-supportive area of concern* *5-7= coaching needed* ***2-4=RTI supportive***
Cluster 6 **Teaming**	**10, 21** ***8-10=RTI supportive*** *6-7= coaching need* *2-5=non-supportive, an area of concern*	**1, 4, 6** *Total of 12-15= non-supportive area of concern* *7-11=coaching needed* ***3-6=RTI supportive***

Note: High scores on belief statements that ARE supportive of Behavioral RTI indicate receptivity; Low scores indicate probable staff resistance to change

High scores on belief statements that ARE NOT supportive of Behavioral RTI indicate probable staff resistance barriers; Low scores on these items indicate staff probably are receptive to change.

Item-by-Item Analysis

Statement	Supportiveness	Cluster of Core Beliefs
1	Non-supportive Belief: BARRIER	Not consistent with Cluster 6: Importance of collaborative "communities of practice" or "professional learning communities" as well as an RTI team in supporting behavioral change
2	Supportive Belief	Consistent with Cluster 1: Purpose of schools and teaching
3	Non-supportive Belief: BARRIER	Not consistent with Cluster 4: How behaviors of students are best changed
4	Non-supportive Belief: BARRIER	Not consistent with Cluster 6: Importance of collaborative "communities of practice" or "professional learning communities" as well as an RTI team in supporting behavioral change
5	Non-supportive Belief: BARRIER	Not consistent with Cluster 2: Relationship of environment and instruction to behavior problems
6	Non-supportive Belief: BARRIER	Not consistent with Cluster 6: Importance of collaborative "communities of practice" or "professional learning communities" as well as an RTI team in supporting behavioral change
7	Supportive Belief	Consistent with Cluster 2: Relationship of environment and instruction to behavior problems
8	Non-supportive Belief: BARRIER	Not consistent with Cluster 5: Responsibility for change lies with whom?
9	Non- supportive Belief: BARRIER	Not consistent with Cluster 4: How behaviors of students are best changed
10	Supportive Belief	Consistent with Cluster 6: Importance of collaborative "communities of practice" or "professional learning communities" as well as an RTI team in supporting behavioral change
11	Non-supportive Belief	Not consistent with Cluster 3: What the student is entitled to receive in a classroom
12	Supportive Belief	Consistent with Cluster 2: Relationship of environment and instruction to behavior problems
13	Supportive Belief	Consistent with Cluster 3: What the student is entitled to receive in a classroom

Statement	Supportiveness	Cluster of Core Beliefs
14	Non-supportive Belief: BARRIER	Not consistent with Cluster 1: Purpose of schools and teaching
15	Supportive Belief	Consistent with Cluster 5: Responsibility for change lies with whom?
16	Non-supportive Belief: BARRIER	Not consistent with Cluster 1: Purpose of schools and teaching
17	Non-supportive Belief: BARRIER	Not consistent with Cluster 4: How behaviors of students are best changed
18	Supportive Belief	Consistent with Cluster 5: Responsibility for change lies with whom?
19	Supportive Belief	Consistent with Cluster 4: How behaviors of students are best changed
20	Supportive Belief	Consistent with Cluster 3: What the student is entitled to receive in a classroom
21	Supportive Belief	Consistent with Cluster 6: Importance of collaborative "communities of practice" or "professional learning communities" as well as an RTI team in supporting behavioral change
22	Non-supportive Belief: BARRIER	Not consistent with Cluster 3: What the student is entitled to receive in a classroom
23	Non-supportive Belief: BARRIER	Not consistent with Cluster 5: Responsibility for change lies with whom?
24	Supportive Belief	Consistent with Cluster 3: What the student is entitled to receive in a classroom
25	Supportive Belief	Consistent with Cluster 4: How behaviors of students are best changed
26	Non-supportive Belief: BARRIER	Not consistent with Cluster 2: Relationship of environment and instruction to behavior problems
27	Non-supportive Belief: BARRIER	Not consistent with Cluster 2: Relationship of environment and instruction to behavior problems
28	Non-supportive Belief: BARRIER	Not consistent with Cluster 4: How behaviors of students are best changed
29	Supportive Belief	Consistent with Cluster 1: Purpose of schools and teaching
30	Non-supportive Belief: BARRIER	Not consistent with Cluster 1: Purpose of schools and teaching

Note: The author would like to thank Lodi (Calif.) Unified School District's Secondary Schools, TAASA (Through Adaptations, All Students Achieve) team leaders, principals, and vice principals for their insightful comments over the last three years on school belief barriers to academic and behavior success. This was the catalyst for development of belief system assessment tools in academics and behavior. Research on shifting belief system is currently in progress, Diana Browning Wright, TAASA Director.

155

References

Crone, D. A., & Horner, R. H. (2003). *Building positive behavior support systems in schools: Functional behavioral assessment.* New York: Guilford Press.

McIntosh, K., Chard, D. J., Boland, J. B., & Horner, R. H. (2006). Demonstration of combined efforts in school-wide academic and behavioural systems and incidence of reading and behaviour challenges in early elementary grades. *Journal of Positive Behaviour Interventions, 8,* 146-154.

Sadler, C. (2000). Effective behavior support implementation at the district level: Tigard-Tualatin School District. *Journal of Positive Behavior Interventions, 2*(4), 241-243.

Sprague, J. R., & Golly, A. (2004). *Best behavior: Building positive behavior supports in schools.* Longmont, CO: Sopris West Educational Services. *www.sopriswest.com.*

Sprague, J. R., & Walker, H. M. (2005). *Safe and healthy schools: Practical prevention strategies.* New York: Guilford Press.

157